Costume Society of America series

Phyllis A. Specht, Series Editor

Managing Costume Collections

An Essential Primer

Louise Coffey-Webb

Foreword by Robin D. Campbell

Texas Tech University Press

This book is typeset in Minion Pro. The paper used in this book meets the minimum requirements of ANSI/NISO Z39.48-1992 (R1997). ∞

Cover photograph/illustration: Angels Costumes London.
Photograph by Louise Coffey-Webb, with permission.

Library of Congress Cataloging-in-Publication Data
Names: Coffey-Webb, Louise, author. | Costume Society of America.
Title: Managing costume collections : an essential primer / Louise
Coffey-Webb ; foreword by Robin D. Campbell.
Description: Lubbock, Texas : Texas Tech University Press, 2016. | Series:
Costume Society of America series | Includes bibliographical references
and index.
Identifiers: LCCN 2015039969| ISBN 9780896729575 (paperback) |
ISBN 9780896729568 (hardcover) | ISBN 9780896729582 (e-book)
Subjects: LCSH: Costume museums. | Museums—Collection management. |
BISAC: DESIGN / Textile & Costume. | DESIGN / Fashion.
Classification: LCC NK4701.8 .C64 2016 | DDC 706—dc23
LC record available at http://lccn.loc.gov/2015039969

16 17 18 19 20 21 22 23 24 / 9 8 7 6 5 4 3 2 1

Texas Tech University Press
Box 41037 | Lubbock, Texas 79409-1037 USA
800.832.4042 | ttup@ttu.edu | www.ttupress.org

This book is dedicated to all those along my path, who recognized my passion for costume and its place in our world, and who encouraged me to continue in my pursuits.

Contents

Chapter 3

Illustrations

Foreword

In keeping with the Costume Society of America's mission *to stimulate scholarship in the rich and diverse field of costume and to disseminate information on dress and appearance, i*n 1999 we partnered with Texas Tech University Press (TTUP) to establish the CSA publication series. Since then, the CSA Series has published outstanding work on various aspects of dress and culture. This book by Louise Coffey-Webb represents a major step in a direction that the CSA Series has hoped to take since TTUP brought forth Margaret Ordoñez's *Your Vintage Keepsake: A CSA Guide to Costume Storage and Display.* Focusing on the care and management of garments found in a wide variety of collections—some intended for preservation, others for active use—this work represents the sort of outreach that CSA has long considered a pillar of its mission.

I had the privilege of reading several early drafts of this work as a manuscript and am delighted that it is now making its way into the wider world and into the hands of a ready audience among the numerous museums, historical societies, and rental companies. So many organizations coping with costume collections or holdings have little or no in-house expertise to manage or care for them.

The Costume Society of America has long endorsed the proper care and handling of garments and related articles of clothing. Each year in conjunction with the annual symposium, volunteers donate their time in support of the CSA Angels Project. This one-day event provides conservation, storage, collections management, and curatorial assistance to a costume collection at a small institution, precisely the type of organization that can benefit from this book. Drawing on her vast experience working with both museum and film costume collections, Louise Coffey-Webb takes the time to explain not only what must be done to manage a costume collection but more importantly *why*.

In a voice as engaging as her passion for costume collections, she offers readers advice in an accessible, easy-to-follow format. This is especially vital for smaller, possibly volunteer-run, historical organizations whose members want to provide the very best care they can for their collections but have no professional museum training. Searching for guidance can be prohibitively time-consuming, not to mention frustrating, but now *Managing Costume Collections* is indeed an essential primer for any nonspecialist wanting a short course in implementing the best practices circumstances might allow. Rental companies and others responsible for costume collections in the performing arts have plenty to rejoice about as well. Indeed, it is not just smaller organizations that will find this book useful. Large organizations with well-trained staff frequently look for new and cost-effective ways of doing business, and the information in this book can be adapted to suit any situation.

Priceless in its practical and cost-considerate solutions, this guide should also become required reading in numerous museum studies programs across the country and beyond. It will prove invaluable to students, many of whom will be confronted with clothing and textile holdings when they accept their first jobs in organizations with limited budgets. I wish that it had been available when I worked as curator for the New York State Bureau of Historic Sites. At least two or three times a year I'd receive phone calls from emerging professionals looking for a book that they could show to their board and say, "See, this is the industry standard. We need to do this." Now they have it.

I am delighted to welcome this book to the CSA Series.

Robin D. Campbell, Ph.D.
President, Costume Society of America (2012–2014)

Acknowledgments and Photography Credits

Many thanks to the institutions and private and commercial collections with whom I have consulted, or who have allowed me to observe their storage and even take photographs. Many have been most understanding of the points I tried to make in the text and allowed me to use technique examples that may have since been replaced, so I heartily salute their homage to education rather than being overly concerned purely with their institutional representation. I particularly thank the Academy of Motion Picture Arts and Sciences, Margaret Herrick Library; American Textile History Museum, Massachusetts; Angels The Costumiers, London; Bata Shoe Museum, Toronto; Gabriella and Leo Beranek Textile Conservation Laboratory, Boston Museum of Fine Arts; Charles E. Young Research Library Special Collections, UCLA; Chicago History Museum; Cirque du Soleil, Montréal; the Colonial Williamsburg Foundation, Virginia; T. B. Walker Foundation Textile Education Gallery at the De Young Museum, San Francisco; FIDM Museum at the Fashion Institute of Design & Merchandising, Los Angeles; Hartford Stage Costume Collection, Connecticut; Fashion Resource Center, School of the Art Institute of Chicago; Costume and Textiles Department, Kent State University Museum, Ohio; Los Angeles County Museum of Art; Mathers Museum of World Cultures, Indiana University; Costume Museum & Research Library, Stephens College, Missouri; Western Costume Company; and Woodbury University Fashion Study Collection, California.

Special thanks to individuals with whom I have consulted on specific topics: Linda Baumgarten, Shannon Bell-Price, Gillion Carrara, Anne Coco, Linda Eaton, Michelle Webb Fandrich, Sylvie François, Esther Ginsberg, Dale Gluckman, Sara Hume, Deborah Kraak, Edward Maeder, Catherine McLean, Margaret Messick, Wayne Phillips, Sally Queen, Nancy Rexford, Sandra Rosenbaum, Susanna Sandke, Sharon Shore, and of course, Phyllis Specht, the Costume Society of America Series editor, who first approached me with the idea.

Thanks also go to former editor Judith Keeling, who believed in this project from the start, Joanna Conrad, who replaced Judith upon her retirement, and managing editor Amanda Werts, who guided me meticulously through the final stages of publication.

Photographs

All photographs are used with permission and were taken by Louise Coffey-Webb, unless otherwise noted in the captions.

Introduction

This book is designed to help improve the management of costume collections found in a variety of settings, including smaller museums, historic houses, historical societies, colleges, universities, rental companies, theaters, corporate archives, theme parks, vintage retail stores, or private collections. As costume collections are inherently fragile, it is inadvisable to exhibit (or use) them for long periods, which results in most of the collection requiring long-term storage. Appropriate storage is costly, and it has been found that even well-budgeted institutions may not always share the wealth evenly among their collections. Although the study and display of costume is now firmly on the radar, and costume exhibitions are now often the most well-attended, costume collections historically held less status than most other collections. Hence today, some collections may need to battle for resources within their institutions. Times are changing; for example, with the Metropolitan Museum of Art's "Alexander McQueen: Savage Beauty" exhibition, 661,509 visitors attended, making it the eighth-most popular show in the museum's nearly one and a half centuries, and none of the other top shows were about costume or fashion. Internationally traveling costume exhibitions are again on the rise. Although unquestionably expensive, demand is such that all the necessary arrangements are being made to enable such cultural exchange and enjoyment.

This is not a simple "how-to" book, because anyone dealing with a costume collection knows there are no simple answers to the many challenges (financial, physical, intellectual, or political) that face a costume custodian. However, it does address issues that anyone caring for a collection needs to understand to arrive at optimal solutions. Consequently they may form their own answers to their various challenges. The purpose of this book is to provide a holistic approach to problem solving—a "hands-on pedagogy," if you like. Drawing on years of academic research and personal experiences with both public and private costume collections, I discuss a range of techniques for costume organization, maintenance, care, storage, and outreach. Whether the goal of your collection is preservation, education, or making a profit, it behooves you to maintain your assets—your costumes.

Costume collections differ in many ways from other historical objects owing to the nature and malleability of their construction and components. Readers will discover many flexible and creative ideas in this book to overcome obstacles of cost, policy, pressure from donors, and so on. While seeking to promote the accepted "preservation gold standard," alternative solutions are presented so that even when the gold standard is unattainable, a baseline level of care exists to counter any manager's set of personal constraints.

In order to understand the typical vocabulary used in connection with preservation and costume collections, a complete glossary is provided, as well as sample forms and useful resources in the appendices. Also you will find information on the Costume Society of America's well-regarded "Angels Project," which helps smaller collections with their preservation issues.

A word about the use of the descriptor "costume": Language is quixotic, and as material culture historians well know, words can change their descriptive meaning over time. The word "costume" is one such example. It was the accepted term for historical clothing during the twentieth century. Indeed, both the Costume Society (UK) and the Costume Society of America, formed for the serious study of dress worldwide, attest to that. There have been many attempts to explore the use of a more suitable word, but none has yet been found upon which the majority can agree. Europe seems to have taken a next step: The preeminent Victoria and Albert Museum in London has recently changed its departmental descriptor from "Dress" to "Fashion." Most US museums, however, still use "costume." There is understandable confusion when differentiating between garments designed for everyday wear and those designed for performance, also referred to as "costume." As this book addresses all manner of garments, the author has chosen to retain "costume."

Managing Costume Collections

Chapter 1
What Is Collection Management?

Implementing a Management System

Costume collection management is a system of organization to enable you to accomplish a number of goals with the collection under your stewardship.

Logically, the person in physical charge of a collection is often called a *collection manager*. However, due to cultural or professional differences, the person in charge may also be referred to as a *keeper* (UK), a *curator*, or sometimes a *registrar* or *conservator*. Whatever your title, if stewardship of the collection is your responsibility, in my book you are a collection manager.

For the purposes of this book, it is assumed that the reader is responsible for the maintenance and protection of a costume collection, be it for as few as a dozen items within a larger museum collection, to many thousands of costumes in a rental company. Your stewardship will either place you as the decision-maker with regard to the available resources of time, labor, and budget, or it will necessitate informing and persuading others who control the resources you require. While the term *collection manager* may not garner the cachet of the term *curator*, it is arguably as important a position. If the study of material culture as it pertains to apparel throughout history is your métier, then access to the objects, and records of all their supporting context, is the altar of your knowledge. Primary sources reign, and those researchers whose main references are other people's writings and theories, rather than the clothing itself, may be missing rich and valuable resources while bypassing the actual materials.

Cathy Ritchie, collections management advisor for the Government of Yukon, Canada, posted a statement that clearly summarizes the responsibilities:

> When caring for collections, we are often caring for objects from the past, but as the caregivers to those collections, we must always be thinking of the future. Decisions we make, how we handle, document, exhibit, and store objects impact their future. Thus we want to make careful and informed decisions about the collections entrusted to our care to ensure that they are safe, secure and meaningful not just for the next exhibit or for the next few years, but for future generations. (www.connectingtocollections.org, January 18, 2013)

Any costume collection, whether in a nonprofit institution primarily focused on preservation and education, or in a rental company primarily interested in entertainment and profit, will benefit from attention to maintaining its assets. Thus begins the journey of assessment and understanding that becomes the groundwork for managing the assets in your charge. Following are some procedures to make your stewardship easier.

Goals, Inventories, and Collection Policies

Identifying the Type, Scope, and Purpose of Your Collection

How do you set about identifying or creating a system of organization? Before even taking inventory, discover and identify the type, scope, and purpose of your collection. In other words, understand the goals:

- What is the reason for your collection's existence?

- What is its function?

- Is there a mission statement? And if so,

- How are the goals of the collection defined?

However, if you cannot answer these questions, you may take an inventory first. Having a summary of your holdings will help determine its function. For example, you may be surprised to discover that you have a huge collection of hats, or an emphasis on one particular designer. These discoveries could influence your future collecting patterns as well as your goals. If you have trouble identifying your goals, think about the driving force behind the collection's formation. If, for example, you have a rental costume collection, your purpose is to serve customers needing to find period or character clothing to fit today's woman, man, or child. It is advisable to create a mission statement for your business even if you are a commercial establishment. It is good business practice to declare your mission statement on whatever materials are disseminated, such as your brochures, website, and even invoices. For a long-range business strategy, you might consider a vision statement to include your dreams and goals beyond your current function. If, on the other hand, you have a university collection to be used as a teaching tool for students, your scope and purpose could be very different, because if the clothes do not need to be worn, there will be less concern about size or sturdiness. If your institution is a museum, its mandate probably includes preserving its collections, and there may be increased interest in quality and rarity. Ask yourself if the focus is on

- Acquiring or collecting

- Preservation

♦Education or the dissemination of knowledge about the collection

♦Distribution of, access to, lending, or renting the collection

If the institution accepts public funds or donations, a transparent mission statement becomes crucial, and the collection's modus operandi can then be supported from an ethical and practical basis.

Managers of costume collections are usually very aware of their collection's particular demands, which is why it is imperative to "know thy collection."

In Valerie Cumming's book *Understanding Fashion History,* the author clearly understands the demands that face managers of costume collections. Her language only cites museum professionals, but the concerns are universal with any type of clothing collection:

> The one fact that invariably surprises researchers and museum professionals without knowledge of dress collections is the huge amount of hands-on labour that curating dress to tolerable standards requires. Preparing detailed inventories, regularly checking stored collections for damp, pests and other hazards, getting out and then returning material required by researchers and students and the preparation of garments for display takes much longer for a curator of dress than for their colleagues who curate ceramics, paintings or furniture. Volunteers and friends' organizations are invaluable allies in the housekeeping aspects of this work, but volunteers cannot be expected to take responsibility for research, exhibitions and education, and all of these have to be fitted around the edges of caring for collections. (70)

Admittedly, other material object collections can also comprise widely varied media, but clothing and accessories are unique in that they fit on or around a body and are therefore malleable in a three-dimensional way. They also overlap, layer, and support other components and need to be coordinated with regard to date and design. Additionally, there may be several different ways to coordinate the components. All of these factors render organization, storage, and display a specialized challenge.

Making an Inventory

Once you have identified the goals of the collection or understood the mission statement, you are now in a position to inventory the collection, if it has not already been done. An inventory is a numerical record rather than a complete catalogue. The numbers can be used for analysis and planning. It is most useful to describe your holdings in a way that makes sense to other decision-makers, such as your board, client, manager, bookkeeper, insurance agent, registrar, or patron. Also consider that they may not be familiar with a costume lexicon. Beyond basically enumerating your objects, ask the questions that will affect space and storage demands, such as:

- How many garments are very old or very fragile, that is, in need of special care?

- How many outfits have two or more parts?

- How many accessories are there? Will they need special supports or boxes?

- How many garments comprise flat textiles, for example, sarongs, saris, or shawls? (This information will be useful in determining whether a garment should be hung or boxed.)

- What about ephemera? Can it be stored flat, or is some of it three-dimensional?

Also make note of how many items are already in boxes, hung, or on shelves. Once you are armed with your goals, mission statement and inventory, you are in a position to create your collection policy, and further, to begin planning your effective system of organization.

Creating Your Collection Policy

Creating your collection policy is a way to publicly communicate your plans and ideas, and, by describing the demography you serve, deciding who has access to your collections. It will declare what you currently collect or do not collect. A statement such as, "We do not collect military uniforms," if that is the case, may save you much hassle. Your policy may also include a declaration on desired condition or provenance, as well as procedures for donation.

It may be helpful to be familiar with the Costume Society of America's Resolution, and consider how to communicate this to your potential customers and patrons. It reads as follows:

> The Costume Society of America acknowledges that clothing is designed and created to be worn. However, with age or associations, clothing takes on particular values and meanings and deserves special care and consideration. The wearing of articles of attire inevitably exposes them to dangers of damage and deterioration; these dangers increase with the age and/or fragility of such articles.
>
> Therefore, the Costume Society of America encourages persons and organizations charged with the preservation of costume to prohibit the wearing or modeling of articles **intended for preservation**.
>
> Further, the Costume Society of America discourages any action which alters the original state of such articles. Since any information related to the provenance, condition and treatment of costume enhances the understanding, meaning

and value of an article of adornment, the Costume Society of America strongly urges that all such information should be collected and made available when that article is transferred to another party. (emphasis in original)

Your collection policy needs to be agreed upon by all stakeholders and published in some form, be it in a brochure, annual report, flyers, or your website. If you are having difficulty describing what you do collect or acquire, try thinking of it the other way around. What do you *not* collect? For example, one major Hollywood studio wardrobe company no longer specializes in children's clothing. On the other hand, it has most of the market for today's contemporary costume because it produces television programs and therefore has access and need in that area, as compared with a rental company with strength in period costume that serves theater and period film production. Likewise, some major institutions are now declining to collect real fur items, stating insufficient storage, such as cold storage at 40° Fahrenheit (F) and 50-percent relative humidity (RH), which is considerably lower than the general recommendations for costume storage.

It is important to communicate and, indeed, have an ongoing dialogue with other institutions and establishments, so as to understand others' special areas of collecting and expertise. There is no point in competing for the same resources (donors, grants, etc.) in the same geographical area. In fact, there is much benefit to be obtained from collegial relations, such as being the recipient of donations considered inappropriate for another institution about which you may not otherwise have heard.

Deciding Who Has Access

Your collection policy will help you decide who has access to the collection, and it will inform your public of your decision. It will also serve you well when you feel well-meaning donors or administrators twisting your arm to accept a donation. Sometimes there are political situations, such as an honored donor who is planning to leave an estate to the institution, when accepting a few unwanted hats is worth the forthcoming endowment. Thus, often it is not just the public that needs to be made aware of your collecting policies but also your board and development office.

If you represent an educational institution you will need to accommodate researchers and students. If you are primarily in existence for students, they will need to have priority over other callers. After all, they are paying tuition for the privilege. If your institution is publicly funded, then in theory the general public should have access. However, it is a rare museum or historical society that has enough human resources to embrace all callers. For a rental company, a common policy is to provide access only to those researchers with whom they do business. This simply makes good business sense. If you have a private collection, you may feel under no obligation to accommodate researchers. Sometimes it is worth rethinking that policy, as there are innumerable benefits to accommodating all serious inquirers, including the following:

- Learning more about the objects in your collection by adding to your own knowledge; and making arrangements to use the researcher's photographs or a copy of the pattern taken from one of the objects in your collection (Be sure to ask the researcher to share the results of their work.)

- Sparking interest in future donors, interns, or customers

- Creating goodwill in the community

- Opening previously unforeseen doors to expansion

- Requiring that a copy of the research (manuscript, pattern, or book) or production (video, PowerPoint lecture, or sound recording) be added to your library

- Being able to use others' work on your collection as PR for your collection, by arrangement, of course (For example, due to its part in the preproduction research on the film *Bram Stoker's Dracula* [1992] the Los Angeles County Museum of Art's [LACMA] Doris Stein Research Center was a credited resource for costumes that appeared in the film.)

- Networking with your researchers' contacts

An example of a combined mission statement/collection policy comes from the Woodbury University Fashion Study Collection:

> Furthering the University Mission to prepare graduates as articulate, ethical and innovative life-long learners, the Fashion Study Collection serves to enhance the learning experience of all interested students and serious researchers by collecting objects pertaining to all aspects of dress (with particular emphasis on California) in order to study, display, and preserve the history, manufacture, and craftsmanship of clothing, adornment, and textile production. Criteria for accepting objects include the consideration of appropriate quality, timeliness, duplications, authenticity, condition, alterations, additional supportive documentation, and space availability.

Following is an example of a policy for Western Costume's special rental costume collection referred to as "The Collection." It comprises many historic objects originally from the outstanding Southern California collector Helen Larson.

The Collection at Western Costume Company
POLICIES

> The Collection is truly one of a kind and is an invaluable resource to the costuming community. Helen Larson tended

to her treasured collection with a velvet touch. In true Helen Larson tradition, we are committed to upholding the standards that Helen set forth years ago. With this in mind, please adhere to the following policies:

- There is to be no cutting of Collection garments in any way. Alterations including style change, size change, the removal of fabric and/or trim will require approval from the Collection Supervisor.

- Any garments that have been altered without approval must be restored and returned to The Collection in their original size and form.

- Aging and over-dyeing of garments is not permitted without Collection Supervisor approval.

- Do not write on, remove, or alter labels in any way.

- All items must be returned as they were sent out. For hanging items this would be on a tissue padded hanger, a wood suit hanger or a skirt/pant hanger. (A charge of $7.50 per hanger will be assessed for each item incorrectly returned.)

- Damages, repairs and restoration are the responsibility of the production company. Responsibility takes effect at the time of pick-up or shipment and ends upon assessment by the Collection Supervisor at time of return.

- All repairs should be made prior to clothing being returned to The Collection. If items are returned and repairs are needed you will be notified of the repair and the time it will take to complete the job. We will request a PO and bill the production company.

- The replacement fee for items lost from The Collection is a minimum of 15 times the production rental rate, unless otherwise specified prior to pick-up or shipment.

- A charge of $150 will be applied to each lost matching belt.

- Cleaning is the responsibility of the production company. (We have a list of approved cleaners.)

- Costume rentals returned to The Collection in shipping containers, which require pressing, will be sent to the approved cleaners at the production company's expense.

- All possible care must be taken to protect wardrobe against fading from sun exposure and over-head lighting.

Thank you for choosing The Collection at Western Costume Company.

Organizational Systems

General Organizational Systems Examples

Your guiding goal is to organize your collection in a way that makes sense for its use and purpose, while preserving your assets. The "preservation gold standard" would ideally preserve your collection to the optimum extent possible, without prohibiting accessibility or the fulfillment of the collection's stated purposes. What it may not incorporate are the everyday challenges, as described by Valerie Cumming, that result from any number of restrictions, such as physical or financial. Following are some examples of various costume collections with different end uses. These examples may not be optimal, but they serve to introduce varied approaches based on systems in place to facilitate access or preservation. You may recognize some of these techniques and systems, and you may also have your own ideas for improvement.

The Hartford Stage Company's theatrical costume collection in Hartford, Connecticut, employs organizational methods that are fairly typical for collections used in productions and worn by actors.

Racks are consequently arranged by type of garment, sex of wearer, size, and color. While this system works for costume designers who are looking for specific garments in specific colors and sizes, the racks are typically overcrowded due to lack of space. Pulling from an over-crowded rack will abrade the garments on either side. Also, the commercial white plastic dividers (seen in 01-001), though easy to view from the aisle and long enough to effectively divide the garments, are not archival and will probably emit chemical gas over time. (This deleterious effect is known as off-gassing.) Note that a number of gadgets designed for the apparel industry could well serve costume collections if only they were made of inert materials.

01-001: Men's jackets organized by size and color, using plastic garment industry rack dividers. Hartford Stage Costume Collection. Photograph by Louise Coffey-Webb, with permission.

Rental companies may not be so concerned about preservation, but eventually the disintegration of the garments will prevent their being chosen for productions, and therefore the companies will be unable to reap remuneration. Also, those unwanted garments will encroach upon otherwise useful storage space.

The living history museum of Colonial Williamsburg in Williamsburg, Virginia, has, as of the early twenty-first century, a collection of approximately thirty-five thousand garments in circulation, worn by the reenactors each day, and a further twenty-five thousand in storage. A collection of this size must have an efficient method of retrieval, including

- Type of garment

- Size of garment

- Fiber content (listed in order: cotton, wool, silk—presumably representing the season or social strata)

While most garments are hung for accessibility and use typical dry-cleaner's automated electric racks, petticoats, shirts, and chemises are folded on shelves rather than hung. This is presumably due to space considerations, as well as the fact that the undergarments may not need to retain their shape as much as the outer garments. An automated dry-cleaner's rack is a good solution in this instance as all the garments are new re-creations and therefore sturdy enough to withstand the jolting and swaying caused by the automated rack. The rack shown in Figure 01-002 has individually numbered slots for each costume.

At Angels The Costumiers in London, England, the storage space is a vast warehouse. Angels is arguably the largest costume house in the world, and this two-hundred-year-old company boasts not only eight miles of hanging costume but also original Elizabethan garments as

01-002: Dry-cleaning-style automated rack for reproduction clothing worn by reenactors in 1992. The Colonial Williamsburg Foundation's Costume Design Center. Photograph by Louise Coffey-Webb with the permission of The Colonial Williamsburg Foundation.

well as other museum-quality antiques. Access to the antique treasures is limited, and they are stored in a separate secure area with dust covers. Designers are allowed, by appointment only, to carefully make pattern copies from the antique garments, which are never removed from the premises. A further deterrent to overhandling would be the duplication of a pattern once made, and creating a library of such patterns for use by future designers. Newer and less fragile garments are stored mostly on racks (see Figure 01-003) by type of garment, male/

01-003: View of the atrium storage area, surrounded by floors of further costume storage. Angels Costumes London. Photograph by Louise Coffey-Webb, with permission.

female, children, period, and occupation (e.g., military). Sometimes racks are retained after filming and still organized by film or television production, for quick retrieval when there might be reshoots after wrapping the production. Other beneficial storage methods might include ensuring that there are UV filters on the light fixtures, timed lighting, effective air-conditioning filters to prevent excessive dust, and some form of humidity control. (This is England after all!) Such environmental measures are more fully discussed in chapter 3, "Controlling the Environment."

The Winterthur Museum in Winterthur, Delaware, is a historic house with an emphasis on decorative arts, with only a small costume collection. It serves as a good example of historic house collection

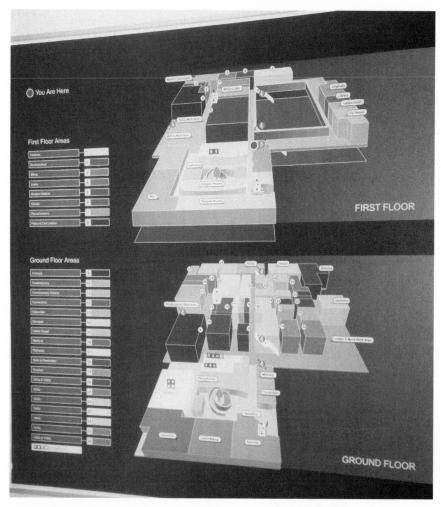

01-004: Wall plan of holdings showing color-coded sections. Angels Costumes London. Photograph by Louise Coffey-Webb, with permission.

challenges. The museum holdings are geared toward rotating interior household displays and are grouped accordingly in storage. In historic houses, anything made of a textile, such as bed coverings, lace doilies, or rugs, is frequently assumed to fall under the costume and textiles collections manager's care. At Winterthur, all furniture slipcovers are stored together, bedcovers are hung on long metal pipes to allow for as little folding as possible, and draperies are draped over poles until they are periodically hung at the windows. There is even an entire wall for storage of trims. No hanging storage is available for the small garment collection, which is stored in the typical costume archival boxes, and identified on the outside of the box with labels. (More about labels in chapter 2.) Pocketbooks and other accessories are stored on shelves in the Needlework Study Room in dark closets; docents guiding tours open the doors occasionally and turn on the lights. Frequently there is a rotation of items displayed in situ, as is customary in historic houses. Displaying objects in separate cases would detract from the benefit of witnessing a slice of contextual history. This is a form of open storage. It is wise to place a barrier between the object and the piece of furniture it is up against; Mylar sheeting works well.

The Study Collection of the Fashion Resource Center at the School of the Art Institute of Chicago supports transdisciplinary curricula. The contents of the collection have been selected to stimulate student creativity. For example, a simple white shirt is hung next to deviations of the basic shirt design. The collection emphasis is on late-twentieth and early-twenty-first-century avant-garde designers. The art school focus at this resource center encourages organizing much of the collection by designer name, and since the garments are mostly less than fifty years old, the preservation issues are not as urgent as they might otherwise be. The Fashion Resource Center is supervised by a director (also an instructor in the program) and an assistant director, and staffed by volunteers trained by the affiliated museum, the Art Institute of Chicago. It is worthwhile observing other institutions' use of volunteers, interns, or work-study students to compare and contrast with your own needs and resources, while weighing up the various pros and cons. Consider the dilemma of the Fashion Resource Center, which, for security policy reasons, is unable to allow students to staff the center. The trained volunteers they do use are usually of retirement age and consequently not permitted to stand on step stools, which effectively means that they do not have access to all the resources.

The Western Costume Company in North Hollywood, probably the largest costume rental house in the United States, has been through many metamorphoses with regard to buildings and ownership. Their vast holdings dwarf any major costume museum, so their collection is stored in warehouses, with double levels of garments that are reached with large industrial rolling ladders. Similar to the Hartford Costume Collection, the Western Costume Company's organization system reflects their users—the designers and costumers who are looking for garments by period, type, size, sex, and color. Consequently, their collection is organized to support "pulling"—the act of creating groups of clothing by actor and scene, usually in quantities greater than will actually be needed.

Today, members of the Western Costume Company's staff are educated in the skills of preservation, as they realize that protecting the longevity of their assets also protects their financial bottom line. For example, Figure 01-005 shows sweaters stored in archival polypropylene boxes, which are more waterproof than the typical costume archival boxes of lignin-free cardboard. Sweaters are stored flat rather than hung, to prevent their knit construction from stretching out, to reduce the collection of dust on the garment, and to reduce light-fading. They are organized by period and color palette (so important for a designer), as well as interleaved with archival tissue. The boxes are clearly labeled, and some have photographs—good for speedy re-

01-005: 1930s sweaters grouped by color in well-labeled corrugated polypropylene archival boxes. Western Costume Company. Photograph by Louise
Coffey-Webb, with permission.

trieval as well as minimizing the handling of garments while in the
process of choosing. Most rental houses simply hang their sweaters over a hanger, often a wire hanger, folded in a triangular fashion, which does alleviate stretching out somewhat, counteracting
the gravitational effect on perpendicular yarns. Wire hangers are not
sufficiently broad to prevent "hanger bumps," as they are the narrow-
est form of hanger, and sometimes they will bend with the weight of
what they are holding. The ideal hanger would be padded with an
inert material. However, space is often an issue while making such
compromising decisions. (See also the "Space Concerns" section of
chapter 3.)

Accessory Storage Systems Examples

Storage for accessories has different considerations and is often physically in a different area from rack storage or boxed costumes. Many
small areas can be adapted adequately for accessory storage, and in
many cases it does make sense to store similar objects together as
their shapes and materials may be similar, such as scarves or gloves.
Beginning with differing approaches to shoe storage, you can see how
semispecialized storage can change over time, from shelves to drawers in compact storage.

SHOES

There are numerous methods of shoe storage, many of which have
changed with time, available materials, space, and knowledge. As an
example, the following shoe storage evolution in the Costume and
Textiles Department at LACMA begins with the latest and best storage method to date: Each shoe is on a separate Ethafoam board for
ease of safe handling and removal from its aluminum drawer. Each
shoe is individually tied with cotton twill tape through a slit in the
board. The placement of the twill tape serves to separate each shoe so
that no abrasion occurs.

The shoes are stable on their boards, so there is no need for tissue
bumpers as shown in Figure 01-007, as these separate boards can be
lifted individually without touching the actual shoes.

Contrast the previous example with the same compact drawer
storage showing an earlier system, divided by very soft abaca fiber
tissue bumpers so as not to rub against the silk of the women's shoes.
Some of the shoes are placed right next to each other, which may result in abrasion when lifted. Also, the drawers tend to shudder a little
when opening and closing. In Figures 01-006 and 01-007, the archival
tags are clearly visible without moving the shoe. This last example is,
however, a huge improvement over another example of 1980s' storage—acidic shoeboxes (see Figure 01-008) with no visuals apart from

01-006: Early-nineteenth-century shoes in compact storage drawer on individual boards. LACMA, 2015. Photograph by Louise Coffey-Webb, with permission.

a very brief written description. The commercial shoeboxes were donated by a local shoe store and gratefully accepted half a century ago. Note the metal-edged cardboard tag, standard issue for museums during the mid-twentieth century. In some cases you may have the original shoebox or even the original receipt and a photo of the donor wearing the shoes. In that case, you should scan the original ephemera and place it near the actual shoes, so that, when looking at the shoes, you realize there are crucial associated ephemera. The original two-dimensional resources may be stored in archival binders and a copy stored inside the shoebox (unfolded and buffered from the footwear).

01-007: Earlier storage version of similar period footwear in compact storage drawer. LACMA, 1987. Photograph by Louise Coffey-Webb, with permission.

If your available display space is limited, consider open storage where items are stored safely but are easily visible; such storage can be in the form of open shelves or pull-out drawers. Figure 01-009 shows a pull-out drawer with footwear held by strips of Mylar. This method has been superseded by the use of encased magnets, as the former method caused unwanted movement when the drawers were opened and closed. These locked drawers at the museum of Colonial Williamsburg are only opened for visitors under supervision. The acrylic cover is inert and easily removed by undoing screws, but the cover still prevents curious fingers from touching, as well as adding an extra dust barrier.

01-008: Shoes stored in commercial shoeboxes, with identifying information typed and taped to the outside. Anonymous collection, 1985. Photograph by Louise Coffey-Webb, with permission.

The Bata Shoe Museum in Toronto, Canada, has another form of open storage, where all the shoes are clearly lined up on shelves, easily viewable while walking through the aisles. Their shoe storage is only open to staff and special guests. Figure 01-010 shows the open shelf storage, with each pair on a pallet. Note the use of twill tape tying the shoes to the board, thus preventing slippage when being moved. In 2006 the Bath Museum of Costume in Britain used exactly this method in its galleries for a public display of eighteenth-century shoes.

The Western Costume Company has begun to store its rental shoes in archival boxes, surrounded by archival tissue. The shoes in Figure 01-011 are stuffed with archival tissue, and pairs are held together

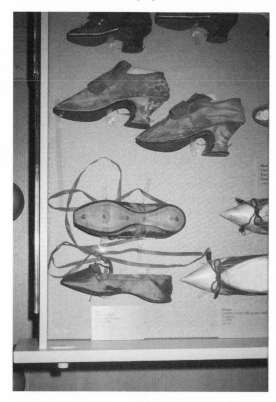

01-009: Study storage drawer under acrylic with former placement method, 1992. The Colonial Williamsburg Foundation.
Photograph by Louise Coffey-Webb with the permission of The Colonial Williamsburg Foundation.

with a rubber band. As you may have experienced upon finding an old stick of chewing gum in your purse, rubber degrades quite rapidly and its detritus may stick to fabric; rubber should thus be avoided. That being said, a rubber band may be preferable to the usual rental company method of poking a giant safety pin through both shoes so that they do not separate, thereby leaving a permanent hole. Twill tape is handy to tie the shoes together. The cost of archival tags can be prohibitive for collections of many thousands of shoes, but improved conditions can be achieved in stages, such as the use of these archival

01-010: Former director Edward Maeder holds the pallet for a pair of eighteenth-century shoes. Bata Shoe Museum. Photograph by Louise Coffey-Webb, with permission.

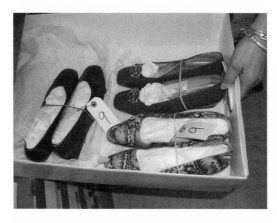

01-011: Shoes in a polypropylene box with size tags. Western Costume Company. Photograph by Louise Coffey-Webb, with permission.

trays, rather than the usual rental practice of digging for shoes in large plastic bins that will off-gas in time. For a rental company, customarily the most important information kept with the shoes is the size, written on a large manila tag. The tag, however, is not archival, and perhaps a smaller archival tag would work just as well. Another idea might be to write the size on twill tape with a permanent pen, forgoing the rubber bands and cardboard tags altogether.

FANS

Fans come in many different shapes, some of which are malleable in that they open and close, and they also exist in a variety of sizes. You have probably seen framed fans and considered the pros and cons of storing them open. Any brisé fan when closed creates folds in the connecting fabric, thus breaking the silk, paper, or vellum over time. Folded fans take up less space and do not collect so much dust. Open fans, however, need to be supported to counteract gravity. An open brisé fan does not have a level base, as the sticks are resting upon each other in a graduating manner, and therefore cannot lie absolutely flat. One benefit to storing fans open is that they can be viewed without much handling. If your fan has its original box and you are choosing to store it open, you need to keep the box in proximity if you care about historical accessorizing. Storing fans in the best possible way for preservation can be extremely time-consuming, as there are no standard shapes, and each support must ideally be custom-made. Framing has its pluses, and the frames themselves can be stored in a drawer or on a shelf out of the light, but it is the most costly solution, as well as restrictive of display possibilities. Consider that you may wish to display your fan cradled in the arm of a dressed mannequin from that era, rather than framed and hung on a wall. Figure 01-012 shows closed brisé fans, with attached archival tags containing a small photograph of the fan in its opened state, thus avoiding the need for overhandling.

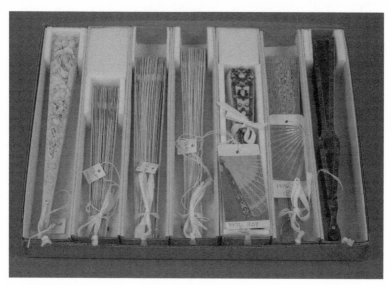

01-012: Fan storage at the Gabriella and Leo Benarek Textile Conservation Laboratory. Museum of Fine Arts, Boston. Photograph © 2016 Museum of Fine Arts, Boston.

01-013: Supported brisé fan at the Gabriella and Leo Benarek Textile Conservation Laboratory. Museum of Fine Arts, Boston. Photograph © 2016 Museum of Fine Arts, Boston.

PARASOLS AND UMBRELLAS

As with fans, storage of parasols can be either open or closed. Stored open they take up more space and consequently may not easily fit in an area that would be away from dust and light. Also, due to the mechanism of the ribs, the fabric takes a lot of strain when fully opened. For this reason, it is not usually advisable to store them open. Again, however, any attempt at softening the creases of the fabric is desired. One method of storage is to lightly stuff archival batting, tissue, or muslin around the central tube, leaving the object semiopen. If this method is chosen, the best approach is to suspend the parasol by its handle or in some way prop it up on its tip or ferrule. You could brace the ferrule by placing it in carved Ethafoam. This helps remove the force of gravity that would occur if it was otherwise resting on a shelf and lying on one side. All these storage methods demand ample space, which is often at a premium. Decisions will need to be made depending on the type and amount of space available. Another method is to store parasols and umbrellas in a drawer, unopened and individually wrapped in archival muslin, tissue, or Tyvek, so that when they are handled, the spokes are less likely to abrade adjacent objects.

STOCKINGS AND KNITS

Due to the construction of knitted garments, hanging is not advised, as the yarns will stretch out and likely become misshapen. (Refer to the angled hanging of the sweaters mentioned earlier.) Quite simply, store knits flat where possible. If you have an original stocking box, you can keep the stockings in there if you use a barrier of preferably archival lens tissue, the edges of which will not catch on a fine stocking knit denier. Some rental companies maintain that, for organizational and accessibility purposes, they must hang the sweaters on racks with all the other garments, cleverly folding them at an angle

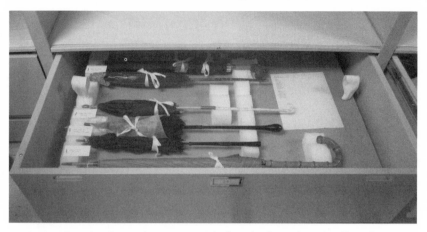

01-014: Drawer of parasols resting on Ethafoam bridges. The Gabriella and Leo Benarek Textile Conservation Laboratory. Museum of Fine Arts, Boston, 2011. Photograph by Louise Coffey-Webb, with permission.

01-015: Hanging parasols in muslin bags. Western Costume Company. Photograph by Louise Coffey-Webb, with permission.

over the hanger bar. While this is certainly not ideal, it is an improvement upon simply hanging the garment straight on a hanger from its shoulders.

COSTUME JEWELRY

In a museum, fine jewelry may be collected and stored in a different department, such as the Decorative Arts Department. Costume jewelry, however, is often kept within a costume collection. It is advisable to keep coordinated sets of earrings, necklaces, and bracelets together, as once they are separated, it seems inordinately difficult to regroup the matching pieces again. Beware of celluloid and separate it from other materials, preferably with Mylar or some barrier without fibers, as celluloid does get sticky and fragile as it ages, and off-gases can harm other artifacts. Drawers lined with archival foam are excellent for brooches, as their pins can be pushed through the foam to avoid movement in the drawer. Costume jewelry used as props to accessorize mannequins usually needs to be accessed by style and color. One very convenient system for storing prop jewelry is a chest of small color-coded drawers (one for necklaces, one for bracelets, one for earrings, and so on) on wheels. You can place archival dividers and foam (such as Volara) as needed in the drawers. The chest can be wheeled to and from the display area.

HATS

As they come in many shapes and sizes, hats cannot always be stored together on a shelf. Some hats may have their original boxes and, as with the fans and shoes, can be stored in those boxes with the appropriate barrier. If a hat is part of an outfit, one suggestion is to store it in proximity to the outfit, rather than with all the other hats. Cirque du Soleil, the international theatrical company based in Montréal, keeps all of its costumes for each production together, rather than separating out all the components by type of material, as a conserva-

01-016: Headdresses and footwear from *Varekai* designed by Eiko Ishioka. Photograph by Marie-Claire Dumoulin. © 2015 Cirque du Soleil.

tor may prefer to do. Storing ensembles by production serves the circus's performance demands (see Figure 01-016). For extremely fragile pieces, a custom box and stand can be made to better support that hat or headdress. Figure 01-017 shows a splendid example of a Chinese headdress in a custom box created by a textile conservator. The cutout handles lift the interior box from the outer box, and the twill tape bows untie so that the headdress can be viewed from all four sides without being touched. This is achieved with the use of drop-down box sides. The box is also clearly marked on the outside, with the accession number and photographs.

01-017: Custom hat box with mount. Photo © Museum Associates/LACMA.

Hats can be kept in boxes on shelves, in drawers, or even suspended on pegboards or vertical wooden dowels. The Chicago History Museum had a form of open storage with their collection of Chicago milliner Bes-Ben hats displayed on shelves in cabinets with sliding glass doors (see Figure 01-018). The School of the Art Institute of Chicago currently uses a pegboard for their study hat collection. The American Textile History Museum created simple but effective crossbar archival cardboard stands to prevent the brims from being crushed.

Storing coordinated outfits together may seem contrary to a very conservative approach to storage based on the ultimate preservation of materials. Evaluate the need for accessibility with that of preserva-

01-018: Hats on shelves with glass sliding doors. Chicago History Museum. Photograph by Stephen Jensen, Chicago History Museum, with permission.

01-019: Easy-access hats on pegboard in the Fashion Resource Center, School of the Art Institute of Chicago. Photograph by Louise Coffey-Webb, with permission.

01-020: Hat storage on enclosed
pull-out shelves, American
Textile History Museum. Photo
by Louise Coffey-Webb, with
permission.

tion. Consider that it may be more important to have complete accessorized outfits in proximity, separated by appropriate archival barriers, rather than individual objects strictly sorted by their medium.
For example, if it matters that a certain nineteenth-century hat was
worn with a uniform, and that you have a photograph of the person
wearing it along with the newspaper article of the event, then these
items should be kept together.

Edward Maeder, former curator of textiles and director of exhibitions at Historic Deerfield, notes:

> It can be historically destructive and impede research to sep-
> arate objects that have been donated as an entity, such as an
> early-twentieth-century wedding box with the complete out-
> fit, accessories, and a ring pillow in compartments within the
> original box. (Phone interview with author, August 3, 2007)

He goes on to say that having to search six different areas for all the related objects is very impractical and would necessitate an up-to-date and effectively accessible cross-referenced record-keeping system. The various coordinated objects and materials can have sufficient barriers yet remain in the original box. Silver, for example, needs to be kept away from silk, to avoid discoloration. If you prefer to keep the items together, the jewelry (for example) might be contained in little custom Tyvek bags, which is easily machine-sewable. When objects get separated and are not sufficiently noted as accessorized outfits, the likelihood of their coming together again, barring an institution-wide inventory or the creation of a new digital database, is very slim. If no foolproof record-keeping is in place, and there has been no responsible party to care for the collection continuously (as frequently happens with smaller collections), it may be hard to know whether there are coordinating wedding shoes or a photograph of the bride to go with the dress.

Often much knowledge resides only in human memory, and it would be unwise to rely on an assistant's personal memory of a donor's story. Volunteers and interns are typically transitory, and institutions can have programs that fall in and out of favor. Consequently, personnel are rarely long term. For this reason, leave a Mylar-enveloped photocopy listing pertinent related information in the box or enclosed in a polyethylene sheet protector from the hanger neck. (One of the three-punched holes fits handily over a hanger hook.) You might note on the tag that the jacket, for example, is part of a three-piece suit. Just putting a letter after the identification number on the tag does not tell you how many items go together when viewing a solitary object. Some institutions list all the accessory letters/numbers on the tag, and simply underline the one referring to the tag's object. (See the "Managing the Records" section in chapter 2.)

Some costume collections are mostly paper and need to be man-

EVENING
WRAP
GOLD, SILVER,
AND SCARLET
BROCADE TRIMMED
WITH BEIGE FOX—
TO BE
WORN OVER
SHELL— NUDE
EVENING
GOWN
WITH SCALLOPED
JEWELLED
PANELS—

ESPECIAL
MISS

DESIGNED FOR
MARION DAVIES
BY
HOWARD GREER
PARIS—

JULY/5-1928

01-021: Howard Greer's sketch and annotations for Marion Davies in the film *Cardboard Lover*, 1928. *Los Angeles Evening Herald*, July 7, 1928. Woodbury University Fashion Study Collection, with permission.

aged and cared for, too. The Academy of Motion Picture Arts and Sciences Margaret Herrick Library in Beverly Hills, California, houses a collection of film costume design sketches. It has been found that when the public, designers, and scholars perform research, they usually search by referencing the designer and then the actor. Thus, the sketch collection is physically organized by designer rather than by film title, production year, or studio. As an example, Figure 01-021 image would be stored with other Howard Greer sketches rather than the title of the film it was drawn for, *Cardboard Lover*. If there is more than one sketch for the actress, Marion Davies, for whom it was created, those sketches would be kept together under the designer's name. They could certainly be cross-referenced with the film title as well.

To summarize chapter 1, as steward of a collection your responsibilities are extremely important in guiding the use, accessibility, and future of the items you manage. Many different systems of organization are available, and they depend on many different criteria, such as available storage space, demands of the institution or the general public, budget, available management tools such as computer databases, and personnel support.

Chapter 2
Record Keeping

Cataloguing

By now you have your inventory, and hopefully you have a computer, because managing a collection in the twenty-first century is a formidable task without one. It is still imperative to keep hard copies of records for security, preferably in more than one location. To date, acid-free paper has a much longer shelf life than a digital disc, and you do not need electricity or monitors to see the records. Consider the necessity of low-tech accessibility during a natural disaster, for example.

The difference between an inventory and a catalogue is a matter of extent of information. A cursory inventory may be sufficient information to apply for a grant, whereas an excellent catalogue can serve as your basis for museum or display label copy, as well as accurate reference material for other publications. In the "Managing the Records" section of this chapter, the pros and cons of many aspects of complete cataloguing processes are discussed. For now we concern ourselves with what is commonly referred to as core or "tombstone" information—admittedly not the most delicate term, but it does capture the essence of the object's meaningful life. The minimal identifying information on the object typically includes the following seven components, if known:

- Object name or type

- Date object was created or modified (e.g., altered)

- Provenance/place of origin as well as destination (e.g., made in China for export to Europe), or previous owners if significant

- Designer, artist, manufacturer, label

- Accession number (the unique number that identifies this particular object)

- Donor/supplier/originator/lender

- Basic description, such as predominant material, color, and design style, which can include a distinguishing feature. (If you are using the "tombstone" information as a basis for label copy, it can be very helpful to include the dominant color or other distinguishing features. There are different styles of display label, and occasionally exhibit labels are grouped together, so as not to impede viewing the display. Sometimes this results in difficulty determining which mannequin outfit is being referred to. The description of a dominant color or distinguishing feature can help in those instances.)

In order to be able to identify the above components, expertise is clearly needed, as well as excellent resources, such as costume history books. Unfortunately, the Internet is not always a reliable resource for such information, as many entries lack expert vetting. It is better to refer to publications by experts that are edited by professionals. In general, avoid self-published works. Let us also remember that when searching a term online, the search results do not differentiate between a blog (opinion) and a scholarly peer-reviewed article (fact). This truly democratic information source requires erudite selectivity.

Cataloguing systems are usually peculiar to each collection and are developed according to their context and priorities. Therefore, customized worksheets are preferable to one-size-fits-all forms. (Sample worksheets for cataloguing are found in Appendix 2.)

The international art world has created a standard for the minimum information needed to identify art, antiques, and antiquities, to aid in their retrieval if stolen. It was developed by the J. Paul Getty Trust in 1993, in collaboration with major international law enforcement agencies, UNESCO, museums, cultural heritage organizations, art dealers and appraisers, and insurance companies, and launched globally in 1997. Since 2004 the International Council of Museums (ICOM) has an agreement with the J. Paul Getty Trust for nonexclusive worldwide use of the Object ID standard. The ICOM website provides a checklist, which includes all the points in the tombstone, although it is more broadly concerned with fine art objects than with costume.

Computer Databases

A computer database management system allows detailed information about an object to be stored and retrieved. This information is known as *data*, and the database is organized to store large amounts of information in a retrievable system, allowing for further additions and searching capabilities. The specific database management system used is referred to and purchased as either application software or a program, as they both do the virtual organizational work for the computer's user. Applications and programs are designed to accomplish specific tasks, such as spreadsheets, worksheets, or cataloguing entries, and their software systems are installed onto your computer's hard drive, which is part of the hardware—or the physical component of your computer. Software is intangible and does not take up physical space. For this reason, it often makes more sense to upgrade software rather than hardware or physical computer components.

A relational database is one in which relationships between the areas of information are explicitly specified by equally accessible attributes or common characteristics. For example, if you search your

database for "red," you may retrieve any red objects, plus any designers with "red" in their name or any technique using that word. The
different areas of information are known as *fields*. Depending on how
you have identified your fields, if you search within a field for "red,"
you will be able to narrow your search, for example, to women's clothing, designers, or manufacturing processes. The application software
used in such a function can be referred to as a *relational database
management system*, and many such systems on the market are specially designed for museums, historical societies, and even theatrical
collections. These products, like everything else digital, are constantly
changing, thus making a particular recommendation very difficult.
There are, however, some variable considerations, depending on
needs, size of collection, and budget, with perhaps the most significant being cost. As of this writing, many costume collections have
worked well with PastPerfect Museum Software. One excellent theatrical costume inventory resource works only with personal computers
(PCs) at the time of this writing, rather than Macintosh computers,
which can be frustrating to many members of the design community
who prefer Apple products. The online Costume & Theatre Inventory
Resources offers a thorough "Costume Piece Worksheet" that could
be adapted to suit your particular needs (see Appendix 1). There are
much bigger, more expensive, and more comprehensive databases on
the market, and you may need to consider one of those if you are a
larger institution with a variety of collections. The good news is that
most new computers today frequently come with a program that you
can easily customize to your own needs, without resorting to the support of an outside company. Two such examples are Microsoft Excel
and FileMaker Pro. Widely distributed since the early 1990s, Excel is
a spreadsheet application using cells arranged in rows and columns
that can be used to sort information. Each row or column could be an
informational field. It also allows for date searching, inventory num-

bers, as well as space requirements, particularly if you include dimensions of your objects. Excel can also alphabetize and create graphs.

To illustrate how fickle the perpetuation of applications or programs can be, take the former Macintosh program called Apple-Works. Unfortunately, AppleWorks no longer exists, and the iWork replacement package (as of this writing) does not seem to be able to create a useable database.

FileMaker Pro is another company that makes database templates for Macs and PCs. FileMaker Pro's subsidiary database Bento was user-friendly, relatively uncomplicated, and easily customized to suit a small-sized collection (see Appendix A). Bento was initially recommended as a replacement for AppleWorks. However, Bento has also been discontinued as of late 2013. All of this software is moderately priced, whereas larger, museum-specific databases cost considerably more.

There is a difference in service quality among the different programs. For instance, Willoughby's program can be custom-designed for your collections. One example of such customization is in the field for dates, where you could insert either "c. 1999," "circa 1999," "1995–2004," or other variations. Conversely, the prepackaged templates available from FileMaker Pro can be very restricting, sometimes forcing you to input a full calendar date, which is usually only possible with a wedding dress—and even then does not accurately record the date of manufacture.

Another factor to consider if you already have some form of database that no longer serves your needs is whether your new program can import your old program without having to reenter all the information. Basically, if your budget is generous, it is recommended to stretch it as far as possible to make good use of the technical support available with your new program. The importance of available technical support, especially by phone, cannot be stressed enough. The reality is that with insufficient staff to devote to a new database, there really is not much time to learn everything new step-by-step or to attend special workshops. Being able to call a specialist every time you reach an impasse is a convenient solution. Many programs offer free trial periods that can be downloaded from the Internet. These are definitely recommendable, so that you can really explore on your own terms before making a purchase decision. If security and access are concerns—in other words, if you would like researchers to use your database—there are ways to lock certain fields to hide information, such as what you paid for a garment or the donor's address.

In sum, if your budget is severely limited, Excel is usually globally available as a standard program, and Excel instruction is widely available at local community colleges and adult schools. Many stand-alone programs will offer a trial use for a short period of time so that you can investigate from an experiential standpoint. Consider whether the company has been in business for a while, is in good standing, and has a reliable technical support system. As changes and updates are constant, it may be very worthwhile to seek advice from other institutions that have already been through the process. There is also plenty of advice and experiential information online. One such resource is the nonprofit Museum Computer Network, whose mission follows: "Helping information professionals use technology to serve their institutions. MCN supports museum information professionals and the greater community by providing opportunities to explore and disseminate new technologies and best practices in the field."

If you are ready to create your own database management system to inventory or catalogue your collection, following is a list of suggested informational fields or categories to include, many of which are described further in the next section of this chapter. Your custom system may work sufficiently well with fewer fields, or you may wish to rename them.

- Sequence number. This is an automatic number that most programs fill in as soon as you begin or open another worksheet or catalogue entry. It notes the number of your entry in pure chronological sequence and has nothing to do with the date of the donation or any other hierarchy.

- Accession number. This number is addressed in the next section and refers to a unique identifier that belongs only to the object you are describing.

- Object title.

- Designer/artist/manufacturer.

- Medium (materials or construction technique) and color.

- Description. Here it is advisable to use as many discrete words as possible for ease of retrieval. Also, it is helpful to describe the purpose or function of the object. Always try to use the correct term, but you may also offer a popular term by which others may search for it.

- Size.

- Date of object/date of creation. Occasionally an object will be made of parts created at different times.

- Provenance.

- Location/where stored. Here you could have a pull-down menu that lists predetermined locations, including unknown. In fact, it is advisable to always fill in a field. That way, you will know what information is known or unknown rather than just surmising that the entry was forgotten.

- Accessories or related but separate components.

- Techniques. These could be pertinent to your collection or the geographical area or to a historical time frame as well as being purely descriptive. You could use, for example, *trapunto* as well as *quilting*, or *feather-stitch* as well as *needlework* or *embroidery*.

+ Donor/buyer/seller.

+ Images.

+ Date entered into database/initials.

+ Conservation/repairs/cleaning.

+ Exhibition/lending/rental.

+ Cost/insurance value/replacement value.

+ Publication record/production record.

Other considerations include whether the worksheet may be printed easily onto one page for manual storage in a binder, or whether a letter of acknowledgment, receipt, or deed of gift can easily be created using information from the worksheet.

The Canada Heritage Information Network (CHIN) has for some years created a collections management software criteria checklist that lists over five hundred function descriptions of criteria to help you decide what aspects of a database management system would be most useful for your collection.

Managing the Records

Whether you use a computer or an index card file, you need to figure out your own system to manage and update information changes, additions, and subtractions. Accuracy is of prime importance, beginning with a numbering system to identify each object uniquely in the collection. A good chapter titled "Managing Collections Information" appears in the book *Registrars on Record*, edited by Mary Case.

Numbering

The purpose of numbering objects is so that each object is uniquely identifiable. In keeping with the principle of Occam's razor (which states that among competing hypotheses, the one that makes the fewest assumptions or is most succinct is the one that should be used), the simplest system is the correct one to use. Most commonly, the first part of the number represents the year the object was acquired or came into the collection, followed by a sequential number unique to the object. Some institutions prefix a letter or two to denote the type of collection, and some have a code number unique to the donor (especially if they are repeat donors). However, some donors change names, or get married or divorced. A common preference is to begin with the year, the unique number of the object, and finally an added A, B, or C for items that belong together, such as two-part suits or belts. If your database does not handle letters and numbers together, you may substitute an extra set of numbers. Many databases are sophisticated enough to be customizable, so this point should not be an issue. Your number system might look like this:

H.2007.0081A-B = "Hands-on" collection item, acquired in 2007, the eighty-first accessioned item that year, a garment with two parts. Or 2008.0010.0005A/D = Four-part outfit acquired in 2008 by donor number ten, the fifth item to be donated that year, of which this tag represents one item out of four total. This particular numbering system uses three sets of four digits. In other words, it allows for 9,999 different donors in one year, plus the same number of objects donated by one donor, which is more than plenty and perhaps rather unwieldy. The uniformity of the digital spacing, however, should guard against the worry of missing or dropping a digit.

Along with being accurate and detail-oriented, be *consistent*. If you begin labeling your left shoe with an "A" and the right with "B," then make that your policy for all left and right objects, such as gloves and stockings. The rule of thumb for adding letters indicating parts to a complete item is a very practical one: If the object itself can be separated, it needs its own letter. That way, if you come across a belt and it is labeled with a "C" following the number, you can identify the outfit with which it belongs. Why use a letter? It distinguishes companionship. Sometimes a letter is underlined to represent that item: 2008.010.005<u>A</u>-D.

When deciding on extra assistance for cataloguing or tagging, please be sure that your volunteer, intern, or worker does not suffer from dyslexia. There was such an incidence at a museum where several hundred pieces of lace were numbered incorrectly, and each item had to be renumbered later, once the issue was discovered. Collections with a long history may have more than one style of numbering system. Experience has taught us that, much as one would like to change everything old and new, it is highly recommended to leave the old numbering system alone and begin newly numbering only recent acquisitions. Too often, any slight imperfection in changing the old system to a new one results in greater confusion—and regret.

Lexicon

Another factor of high importance in cataloguing is your use of *lexicon*—another word for *vocabulary*. Occasionally it is termed *nomenclature*. If you are counting on being able to retrieve a list of objects by type, color, or date, it is important to be consistent with your wording. Categorize objects by general type first, and whether the object would be worn by a man, woman, or child. If the object is a jacket, name it as such, then qualify it with the type of jacket, such as a blazer, bolero, basque—thus, "Woman's jacket, bolero." If you are calling up fields on a computer, you will probably find the records of the desired jacket sooner by asking for a woman's jacket rather than just a bolero. The truth of the matter is that every individual sees clothing slightly differently and subjectively, and the names of clothing vary over time and from country to country. Keeping references simple is advantageous. You can use detailed descriptions, but you will not likely be using those details as main categories.

Various institutions have made gallant attempts at creating lexicons we can all abide by, such as the Getty's Art & Architecture Thesaurus (AAT), Cultural Objects Name Authority (CONA), and Thesaurus of Geographic Names (TGN). The AAT has many historical costume entries, and the TGN is useful if, for example, you are wondering whether to refer to a garment's country of origin as Iran or Persia. The TGN will tell you that Persia became Iran in 1935, so presumably anything created prior to that date can safely be referred to as Persian. The CONA pilot program went live in 2012 and is a structured vocabulary that can be used to improve access to information about art, architecture, and material culture. Another Getty vocabulary is the Union List of Artist Names (ULAN), but their listings are not comprehensive for the fashion and costume world.

Plenty of other publications are available for finding out who's who in fashion. On the other hand, your institution may make a researched contribution to CONA or ULAN, which would be a worthy endeavor if it encourages the perception of clothing as valid material culture for study and artistic consideration. For further information on these vocabularies, please visit the websites listed in Appendix 1.

Some people feel that the subject of clothing has not yet gained its rightful place as a serious study in itself but has tended to piggyback onto other disciplines such as apparel (domestic science/home economics), art history, or material culture studies. Theories from other disciplines are often superimposed onto the study of clothing, while not enough attention is paid to the voluminous amounts of knowledge that can be gleaned from the clothing itself. For this reason, one of the best resources is the International Council of Museums'

(ICOM) own Vocabulary of Basic Terms for Cataloguing Costume, which is available free at the time of this writing. The ICOM Costume Committee, having studied clothing for decades, began work on this vocabulary in 1971. Its goal was to develop a system that would work internationally, applicable "to fashionable and unfashionable dress within the orbit of European style." From this developed the three main categories: Women's Garments, Men's Garments, and Infants' Garments (concluding that garments for girls and boys were covered under women's and men's). The ICOM vocabulary is very straight-forward in its generic terms, with the addition of contemporary or regional terms. Garments are described in relation to the human body, which makes good sense as the body is the one constant factor in all clothing. If, for example, you click on the term "Underwear," you are linked to a three-columned page, with a category number on the left, a description of where on the body the garment is worn, and various different terms. On the right is a simple dotted outline of a woman, with the generic garment outlined clearly. The only caveat for the free download for nonprofit use is that the ICOM International Committee for Museums and Collections of Costume is acknowledged when it is used.

Costume terms are generally hard to codify due mainly to the fact that they follow fashion and the vernacular. New names are created for very similar objects and colors as each fashion period goes by. For example, do we say "hip-hugger," "dropped-waist," or "low-slung"? Plus, clothing can sometimes be worn in different ways. If a shawl is worn as a scarf, a sash, a fichu, or a sarong, is it still a shawl or not, and therefore, what should it be called?

If you are working with a historical society collection, your preferred lexicon tool may be Robert G. Chenhall's Nomenclature, which was originally designed for history museums with American artifacts in mind. It was first published in 1978, and several updates have taken

Vocabulary of Basic Terms for Cataloguing Costume ICOM International
Committee for the Museums and Collections of Costume

Women's Garments	
Main Garments	
1.1 *Covering bodyabove and below the waist* **Dress** (Types 1-6)	
1.11 **Dress (1)** one piece	
1.12 **Dress (2)** two pieces	
1.13 **Dress (3)** three or more pieces	
1.14 **Dress (4)** as 1 to 3 with additional ,optional piece, but complete without it (including dresses with alternativeday/evening bodices)	
1.15 **Dress (5)** one piece needing additional garment forcompletion	
1.16 **Dress (6)** two pieces needing additional garment forcompletion	

Note: The pieces referred to in thisclassification are the main parts of the whole, e.g.**Bodice** and **Skirt** in**Dress (2)**; **Gown, Petticoat, Stomacher** (18thcentury) (3). A trousersuit will be **Dress (2)** if made up of**Bodice**, Pullover and **Trousers**; **Dress (6)** if made up of**Bodice**, waistcoat and **Trousers**. - Such accessories as belt,collar are not taken into account; a separate catalogue entry gives thisinformation.

02-001: Sample page from ICOM International Committee for Museums and
Collection of Costume's *Vocabulary of Basic Terms for Cataloguing Costume.*

place since. Artifacts are divided into eleven categories, with those for costume falling under the "Personal Artifacts" category. The latest version (by Paul Bourcier et al.) is used in the PastPerfect Museum Software.

Finally, a word or two on library systems. Library cataloguing systems have been around longer than those for museums and consequently have developed quite separately. MARC (MAchine-Readable Cataloguing) has been used by libraries for decades and contains sets of metadata structures to facilitate cooperative cataloguing and data exchange. MARC was originally developed to describe bibliographic materials in libraries but has been extended to accommodate related ephemera collections also. I worked with a librarian at Woodbury University who managed to use MARC to describe some couture garments. This was a very exciting exercise because the goal was eventually to create an online library catalogue in which researchers could access everything in the holdings related to, say, Dior, the French couturier. Researchers would be able to see all books, audiovisual materials, slides, garments, accessories, sketches, and photographs of Dior designs within that institution. Perhaps soon it will be possible to connect the databases so that they can all be accessed together.

Dating Objects

Some databases will not accept a mixture of letters and numbers, as in "Circa 1960" or "1960s." You can get around this somewhat by using a range, such as "1960–1969" or "1955–1965." There is a general understanding among published costume historians that "circa" refers to five years before and after the said date. Indeed, the Metropolitan Museum of Art's editorial style guide recommends the interpretation of "circa" as plus or minus five years, and it is officially recognized by the Costume Institute there. It is also advisable when shortening "circa" to use "ca." rather than just "c.," as it is less likely to be confused with any other use of the abbreviation, such as "century." If you are setting up a new database, you can work with your technician or programmer to customize the date field to suit your needs. You may also wish to be able to insert punctuation such as "?" to denote when you are unsure of the date. Sometimes this approach is preferable to simply leaving a blank, which might signify that the information was omitted.

Labels in garments have become a great resource in themselves. One such example: Since the 1970s it has become international law to provide labels denoting the percentage of fabrics or materials in a commercial garment, as well as the country of origin. Since global production has become so commonplace, you may see "Made in the USA of imported fabric." Frequently, imported garments must carry extensive composition and registration labels. Sometimes you may even see tiny embossed metal customs "seals" sewn into the hems or linings, marking (for example) a true Parisian origin to a couture gown.

Another guideline for verifying information is to note that international laws forbidding commercial activity with endangered species have been in effect since the 1970s. For this reason, if you see a new real leopard-skin coat, you can be sure it was not manufactured (legally) in the twenty-first century, but a shabbier example would probably only be as recent as the late 1960s. For more information, refer to the Convention on International Trade in Endangered Species (CITES) website, which includes both flora and fauna.

Measurements

The question of whether to use inches or centimeters can be answered easily, since nearly every other country in the world uses the metric system, and most large institutions and those sensitive to international communication have already changed to metric, it would seem sensible to measure metrically. However, you may also keep a record in inches, but bear in mind that some databases are not set up to record fractions. When photographing an accessory, such as a small purse, child's shoe, or handkerchief, it is customary to use a ruler placed next to the object to help identify its scale or size. With regard to which measurements to take, think about the potential use of these measurements. First of all, they will be used to identify the object, but they can also be used to determine a display mount or mannequin size, and as a way to determine storage needs. It is usual to give the center back (CB) measurement from the neckline seam to the hem, as well as the inseam on pants, crown height on hats, heel height on footwear, and the widest dimensions on flat textiles. When measuring a fringed shawl, be sure to mention whether your measurement includes the fringe or merely the field of the shawl. From a historical point of view, the garment size label may be useful, especially since sizes in the twenty-first century are different from those in the twentieth. Some recent sizes may be a little confusing, such as seeing a size 2 on a garment that turns out to be a medium rather than a very small size. This new sizing is becoming a global standard. Likewise, sizes in Europe are often different. If you work with a rental company or a theatrical wardrobe collection, you may need to ascertain today's relative size for your performer if the garment is from the 1960s, for example.

Visual Images

"One Look Is Worth a Thousand Words." (Fred R. Barnard, *Printer's Ink*, December 8, 1921.)

The prevalence of digital imaging has made it simple to keep object images handy with their descriptions, stored on computers or discs. The recent redundancy of negative film may be a sad loss in the long run. Consider that if a negative has survived from one hundred years ago, it is still possible to develop a positive photograph. However, we

02-002: Makeshift photography studio in collection workroom. Stephens College Costume Museum and Research Library. Photograph by Louise Coffey-Webb, with permission.

may not be able to read images on our current DVD (digital video disc) or USB (universal serial bus) flash drive one hundred years from now. This is not to advocate reverting to conventional photographic film, but rather that we should also print out high-resolution copies on archival paper, so at least they can be scanned again in the future with whatever technology is then available. It is also necessary to retain the original negatives for this reason.

Why are images so important? Certainly images are used for object identification purposes. They are also an excellent and necessary record of condition. Conservators are always taught to document their object photographically before and after treatment, as well as dating when those images were taken. In general, dating every image taken is a good idea, and nowadays, the camera often automatically records the date. A quality set of images can be shown to researchers or interested parties, diminishing the demand for handling the actual object. If cost is a factor, printing in black-and-white is certainly a good alternative, and sometimes the images can be clearer than those found in early-generation digital color images.

Figure 02-002 shows a makeshift photography studio with the requisite roll of paper suspended on the wall for rolling down to the floor in a gradual curve, thereby creating a smooth background without the floor and ceiling lines. Here you see a roll of black paper used as a neutral background to enhance the objects in front. Think carefully about your background color: Often a taupe color (somewhere between beige and gray) will show vintage garments to their best advantage, especially if they include some yellowed fabric or faded lace. A white background has the unfortunate feature of showing up stains and yellowing.

For exhibition purposes, it can generally be assumed that costume aficionados are fascinated by material and construction, and therefore the rendition of a costume's interior construction or a macro-detail of exquisite embroidery can be a wonderful addition to the actual object on display and its didactic label.

An excellent section appears in Robert Thornes et al.'s book *Introduction to Object ID* on how to photograph objects.

Having a photograph of the object (preferably mounted) on the box it is kept in is very useful. At the beginning of the twenty-first century it was still easy to find Polaroid cameras and film. Today, however, everything is digital. The great bonus to Polaroid film was that all you needed was the camera, and you could affix the photograph,

02-003: Archival costume box labeled with photographs. American Textile History Museum. Photograph by Louise Coffey-Webb, with permission.

then and there, on the box, without waiting for development or using a printer. Although Polaroid cameras are no longer with us, there is still a need for immediate renditions of photographs. Consequently, Fujifilm came out with its own digital instant camera. Consider it if you are working under time pressure in an off-site storage space, attic, or basement, where being able to instantly label your boxes with images could be a blessing.

Colors

Describing colors has long been a challenge. Not only do we perceive colors differently, but colors themselves are also a major commercial industry connected with fashion and interiors, and "new" colors are "invented" each season to create new trends. Sometimes, however, these new colors are not so new, but are merely given a more contemporary name or context. This is why using the Pantone Cotton Planner is recommended. With swatches for nearly two thousand colors and identified with a unique number, the planner is rather expensive, but such color guides can be found for much less at online auctions. The Pantone Cotton Planner used to be called the Pantone Textile Color System, and although their systems change names, the Pantone number system is still basically the same and still universally accepted. To test it, I took a hand-held Pantone color paper picker from thirty years ago and looked to see if I could find some matched Pantone color numbers on the online Robison-Anton rayon thread color chart. They did indeed match! Robison-Anton thread cards give their own names and their own "RA" number, but they also list the Pantone numbers—even with their metallic threads chart. While identifying colors of woven garments from woven swatches is easier, a paper swatch can work just as well.

The National Bureau of Standards in Washington, DC, cooperating with the Inter-Society Color Council, put out a Universal Color Dictionary in 1976 that was largely based on the Munsell notations—a color system created by Albert Munsell in the early twentieth century based on hue, value, and saturation. The language component of the publication is helpful in decoding the recommended use of color names, then qualifying them with color adjectives, such as bluish green, purplish pink, and so on. This dictionary is also useful for doing research of early written descriptions, by giving a technical definition for, say, "Alice blue."

There are other coded systems, but Pantone systems are universal and have been around a long time. Today, of course, there are online resources and apps to download, but for textile aficionados, it is so much easier to match fabric colors with real cotton swatches. The adjective descriptors, such as light blue or dark green, are also useful. One museum veteran suggested the use of flora to name colors, such as beet red, eggplant purple, or cornflower blue. There is some logic to this approach, but beware of the many hybrids we see at farmers' markets that would lead to anomalies such as potato blue or bean purple. If you have a volunteer helping with descriptive cataloguing, do be sure that he or she is not color-blind. (This condition is known to affect men far more than women.) In any event, all color recognition is subjective to some degree, so a system such as the Pantone numbers is always useful.

Another important use for the color charts is to measure any light fading. Once while working on the initial Warner Bros. Museum installation, a private lender was anxious about placing his historic costume in the museum for a required six-month period (the usual display time for costumes is no more than three months). We made a record of the matching Pantone color number from various places on the costume and recommended a match checkup every two months to monitor any changes.

Records Maintenance

Your information technology (IT) department, if you have one, might prefer to see a paperless setup with workrooms free of paper piles and files. Doing so is not advised if you are in the business of preserving or maintaining objects. Why is it good to keep hard copies?

1. There may be power outages.
2. There may be system breakdowns.
3. Technology moves on. Perhaps some of you remember when video-tape images were going to be the ultimate records for collections, and how many of you have kept the big floppy discs from when they were the latest thing?
4. Archival or pH-neutral paper has proven to last longer than a disc or other current digital technologies.
5. Consider how you might accurately reflect a hundred-year-old

shop tag with a string tie on a database worksheet, or the signature of a family member on the back of a photograph? These items can be scanned, but their size will inevitably be reduced. You may use a "top-loader" (archival protective sheet) to protect such two-dimensional items and store them next to your hard-copy records. You can also scan those items and keep a copy (similarly protected or in a Mylar sheet) with the actual object to which they refer. This is a good practice to ensure against forgetting any supporting material and as a reminder to check the main files for all related materials.

It is also very important to create a collection procedures manual that outlines parameters, best practices, and record-keeping procedures. Keep everything as a hard copy in an organized manual, such as a three-ring binder, that can easily be pulled off a shelf and referred to without the use of electricity or passwords.

Labeling

Labels

Let us begin by differentiating between labels and tags. For the sake of clarity, a *label* is a long-term method of individual identification, whereas a *tag* is a loose-hanging, often card-stock-weight sign, not intended to be permanent.

The objects in your collection need to be identified with inert labels. Conservators and historical posterity would prefer that they be technically removable. One fail-safe method of long-term documentation is to label the actual object rather than with just a loose tag. Standard practice in the museum field is to permanently write or print the identifying number on a piece of cotton twill tape with a permanent marker, which is then sewn onto the object in a carefully selected location. Attempts have been made to universalize the placement of sewn-in labels, such as costume historian/consultant Nancy Rexford's system from the 1980s. Interestingly, changing styles in exhibitions have influenced their placement. For example, it used to be common to place the cotton label in the center-back neck of a dress, for it was sure to be covered during display. Today, however, there is a marked increase in displaying garments on "invisible" mounts, often allowing the inside of the neck to be seen. To offset this practice, an alternative system is to sew the label in a side seam or waistband instead. Some collections have the label sewn into the hem, but this placement is not recommended. As you can imagine, the label can be very difficult to find if the dress has a voluminous skirt and could require excessive handling. There are three major considerations for label placement:

1. Place the label where it can be easily read. If the dress is stored hanging, it is usually quite convenient to see a label in the neckline.
2. Place the label where it will not distract the eye during display.
3. Place the label on the object in a consistent area (to prevent unnecessary wear and tear on the object while searching for the label).

Tips for labeling are as follows:

- Use a tightly woven narrow twill tape rather than a loose twill or plain weave tape, because it has a smoother surface to write on.

- Use a permanent ink marker, preferably with a retractable tip as a safety measure.

- Let the labels dry a full day before sewing them onto the object.

- When writing the number "7" by hand, use the European style with a line through it, as there is less chance of it being read as the number "1."

- Use capital letters for clarity.

- Rather than cutting and sewing a flat label so that it is attached to the garment on all four sides, reduce the amount of needle invasion to the object by folding over the label and attaching it at only one end. Be sure to use enough tape to fold over and reveal the complete number from one side—that is, double the length of the tape. The loop now provided could be a good anchor for any subsequent tag, again without invading the object itself. It is useful to have a curved or upholstery needle for some hard-to-reach situations.

This is a good project for volunteers with experience sewing.

Precut Tyvek labels are increasingly being used. However, as of this writing, the edges of such labels are rather stiff and might catch on a lace or chiffon collar. (See Appendix 2, "Forms You Can Use: Recommended Label Placement.")

The conservator-accepted method for marking shoes involves the placement of a clear barrier on the sole; followed by the number, which is applied with a dissolvable pigment so that it could be changed or removed if necessary; and finally a top coat. If the sole is black, consider using white pigment. Never write directly on the object without a barrier.

SPECTRUM 4.0 advice document "Labelling and Marking Museum Objects" online from the Collections Trust in the United Kingdom explains how to do this using acrylic polymers and "B72" and "B67," but it is rather complex. If you want to go this route, ask your nearest conservator for advice.

Tags

It has long been the custom in theater collections and costume rental houses catering to production companies to hang a large manila luggage tag from the garment with a large safety pin. The original purpose was quick recognition on a rack, and the fact that the large, black felt-tip script can record the character, act, and scene. Admit-

02-004: Large manila tags are attached with a tag gun. Hartford Stage Costume Collection. Photograph by Louise Coffey-Webb, with permission.

tedly, customary habits are hard to change, but it is far better for the life of the garment to use smaller tags (preferably pH neutral) and smaller safety pins that are pinned in the seams or edges of linings. Even though you cannot control such usage on a production set or trailer, your garments are still likely to spend more time on your rack than elsewhere. Therefore, do what is within your means to improve the tagging method. Figure 02-004 shows the typical use of large manila tags—in this example, attached with a tag gun that shoots a thin line of almost clear plastic through the cloth with a T shape on each end to hold it in place. This is similar to price tags found on clothing

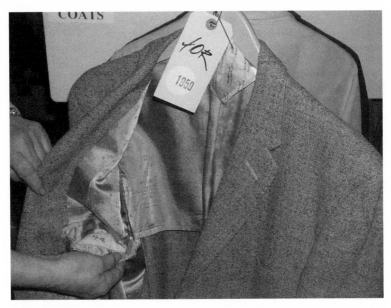

02-005: Man's rental jacket organized by size and date. Western Costume Company. Photograph by Louise Coffey-Webb, with permission.

in stores. The gun has to have enough power to shoot through the end T as well as the line, and although it may not leave a noticeable mark on densely woven men's suiting, it could be detrimental for more delicate or unforgiving materials, such as silk or leather.

Many museums use both archival semipermanent labels and hanging tags on their objects. The main reasons are (1) an instant means of identifying something before the accession process is completed, and (2) ease of identifying the object without removing it from the hanger or turning it inside out.

Face all hanger hooks in the same direction, away from you, because this is easiest for placing on and taking off the rod. It is also customary to have the garments all face to your left. (Whether this

OBJECT NAME
DATE/PERIOD
PLACE OF ORIGIN/ETHNICITY/
DONOR/STUDIO/
PRODUCTION NAME/DESIGNER

ACCESSION /CATALOGUE NUMBER

02-006: Hanging tag sample.

custom had anything to do with reading from left to right, I have no idea.) Consequently, it is typical to place the garment tag on the left armhole or sleeve, where it is easily readable without removing the hanger from the rod. Occasionally one will see a tag attached to the hanger hook itself with a large safety pin, which is less intrusive for the garment. However it does encourage the danger of the tag being separated from the garment when it is removed from the hanger. We see such a technique in Figure 02-005, which shows a hanging non-toxic antimoth sachet (next to the tag) attached with another safety pin. The figure also shows the identifying number sewn into the in-side breast pocket.

Object tags often need to be removable for display, for photography, or for rental purposes. The most popular style that museums and historical societies use with costume and accessories is the two-by-three-inch archival card-stock-weight tag with a punched hole in the upper left corner to allow for a string (see Figure 02-006). The string is usually knotted and attached to a very small brass safety pin. Brass may oxidize over time, but it is inert. The string can be "tugged" so that it stays firm in the bottom loop of the safety pin. Even though the pin is small, it is invasive to the object, so try to pin it into a lining or inside hem at a seam where there are already holes from the sewing thread. Alternatively, the string may be looped through a grommet, a hook eye, or the hardware of a purse, for example. You will need to decide where the least invasive position is, as well as the easiest place to read the tag with little disturbance to the object. Figure 02-006 shows an example of tag information for either a museum piece or a film costume.

Bar Coding

We are mostly familiar with the *universal product code* (UPC) while shopping, as it is a bar-code symbology used throughout the world to identify merchandise. The format was actually invented in 1949 by two engineers: Norman Joseph Woodland and Bernard Silver. After some permutations and redesigns (from bull's-eye to vertical black lines—as favored by supermarket magnate Alan Haberman), it was not until 1974 that the first optical scanner was used to read a pack of Wrigley's gum in Ohio. As early as the 1980s Colonial Williamsburg used this system to keep track of the reenactors' reproduction wardrobes. This was very important with such a large collection, as mentioned earlier. Since these are modern reproductions, they are considered sturdy enough to be dry-cleaned, and the bar-coding system is very helpful in tracking the garments' locations. Many rental houses also use bar-coding systems. The benefits include long-term documentation in a compact format instantly readable by computer. This would be a great time-saver if you are processing many loans, as a rental house might do. For research institutions, a computer-generated use assessment could also be beneficial.

Bar-code labels are typically adhered with heat and glue directly onto the garment. This compromises the integrity and longevity of the garment, which is why museums and other institutions whose pri-

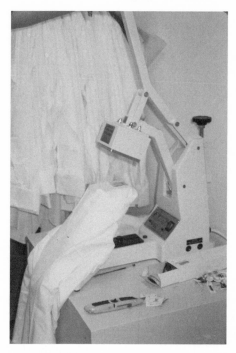

02-007: A bar code being adhered to a man's shirt. Angels
Costumes London. Photo-
graph by Louise Coffey-Webb,
with permission.

mary concern is preservation have not adopted the system. Glue may
permanently damage the object, and museum personnel prefer to add
only reversible amendments to an object. It would be preferable to
use an archival and removable glue, without heat, on historic objects.
Meanwhile, one option could be to glue the bar code onto twill tape
which is then sewn onto the garment in a place where the optical
scanner has access. If such a bar-coded label were separated from its
object, it could be scanned, calling up a photo of the object or other
facts, making it easier to return it to its proper garment. In mannequin displays, there are frequently many layers of garments and accessories to create the complete image, and sometimes card-stock-
weight tags need to be removed for aesthetic reasons. Photographic

documentation is probably the best way to record a completed outfit for the record and for future display.

Interestingly, many established costume rental companies have inherited somewhat loose exchange policies. For example, if an assistant marks out the rental of "one early-twentieth-century-style man's shirt" and the production company loses or destroys it, it can be perfectly acceptable to return another early-20th-century-style man's shirt. Remember, we are talking about a business and the innate value of a rental rather than the object itself.

What if that particular shirt was an authentic one from 1905, custom-made of fine cotton and superior quality craftsmanship . . . and it was replaced with a new poly-cotton collarless shirt? That's a major decrease in the value of the holdings. A bar-coding system could make such a transaction more apparent quickly, and therefore more protective of the assets. Now a lost shirt will need to be accounted for, and charged and insured accordingly.

A word about conventional tags: Sometimes you must remove a hanging tag, as in preparation for display, study, or photography. Where does one put the removed tag? If it is pinned to a bulletin board, in a month you will have forgotten what it was for. One recommendation is to "date-flag" it and create a check-sheet for object removal or deinstallation, reminding you to replace it. Whatever your system, keep it simple and consistent.

Acquiring and Accessioning

Acquiring and accessioning are purposely grouped together, as experience has taught that the accessioning process needs to begin as soon as an object is acquired. For instance, many of you may have hurriedly hung a prospective donation on the back of your office door, swearing that you would never forget the details of its arrival, when all of a sudden, months have gone by with other deadlines, and you simply cannot remember whose great-grandmother the garment belonged to. You can avoid this mistake by having hangtags ready in your top drawer, and indeed in every working area, with string and miniature safety pin attached. Immediately notate the date of arrival, the donor, and any other pertinent information in pencil on the tag and attach it to the object. The donor must also receive a temporary receipt right away. You can replace the tag with neater or further information later.

You may devise any number of systems to record the arrival of objects. A computer database will be most useful. However, from a physically practical point of view, a simple central information depot is recommended. It could even be a binder with lined sheets that is easily grabbed and filled in. A bound register is a permanent record whose pages cannot be removed. So, wherever the object is received, be it in your car or at a luncheon, a stopgap record is readily notated. It is strongly recommended to gather as many details as possible from the donor to aid with your cataloguing process (see the "Cataloguing" section in chapter 2).

Helpful Background Information to Ask the Donor

- Are there any photographs of the garment being worn? If so, offer to have the photograph professionally copied so that the original can be returned to the donor.

- Have there been any known or evident alterations?

- Was the garment made by a family member, dressmaker, or other?

- Where was the garment acquired, found, or purchased?

- What special event was the garment worn to, and what was the date?

- What was the occupation of the wearer/owner?

- Where did the owner live at the time?

✦Were there any other items that were always worn with this garment?

Internal Revenue Service (IRS/Tax Services)

Part of the process of acquiring and accessioning has been discussed previously, with collections policies, numbering systems, record-keeping devices, and so on. If you are with a nonprofit institution, you should be familiar with the requirements of the Internal Revenue Service (IRS). Gathering information has become so much easier now that the IRS has endless documents and forms online. Each year changes are made, and in general, rules are tightened with regard to charitable donations. You can go to the IRS website and find examples of a written acknowledgment for contributions, such as the one excerpted here, current as of 2013:

Written Acknowledgment

Requirement

> A donor cannot claim a tax deduction for any single contribution of $250 or more unless the donor obtains a contemporaneous, written acknowledgment of the contribution from the recipient organization. An organization that does not acknowledge a contribution incurs no penalty; but, without a written acknowledgment, the donor cannot claim the tax deduction. Although it is a donor's responsibility to obtain a written acknowledgment, an organization can assist a donor by providing a timely, written statement containing the following information:
>
> name of organization
>
> amount of cash contribution

description (but not the value) of non-cash contribution

statement that no goods or services were provided by the organization in return for the contribution, if that was the case

description and good faith estimate of the value of goods or services, if any, that an organization provided in return for the contribution

It is not necessary to include either the donor's social security number or tax identification number on the acknowledgment. There are no IRS forms for the acknowledgment. Letters, postcards, or computer-generated forms with the above information are acceptable. An organization can provide either a paper copy of the acknowledgment or electronically, such as via an e-mail addressed to the donor.

Contemporaneous

Recipient organizations typically send written acknowledgments to donors no later than January 31 of the year following the donation. For the written acknowledgment to be considered contemporaneous with the contribution, a donor must receive the acknowledgment by the earlier of: the date on which the donor actually files his or her individual federal income tax return for the year of the contribution; or the due date (including extensions) of the return. (Charitable Contributions: Substantiation and Disclosure Requirements, Internal Revenue Service, Publication 1771 [Rev. 7-2013] Catalog Number 20054Q)

For donations valued at over five thousand dollars for which the donor wishes to take a deduction, IRS Form 8283 will need to be filled out by the donor, an appraiser, and the charitable organization. This form and instructions are available online.

Deaccessioning

Deaccessioning refers to the decision to dispose of some parts of a collection, and really only applies to nonprofit institutions and those held in the public trust. If a donor has given you objects to preserve, display, or teach with, and if they have taken a tax deduction for the donation, there are possible legal implications if those objects are removed from your collection. However, items are deaccessioned all the time, so how is it done? First of all, what are your reasons for deaccessioning? Some possible reasons follow:

- Impingement of storage quality by overcrowding

- Duplication of object

- Irrelevance of object to the collection policy

- Not useful to education objectives

- Similar objects received with more important historical associations

- Similar objects received that are in better condition

- Introduction or discovery of an alternative collection whose collection policy is more closely aligned with the objects

- New knowledge about the ownership of the object that changes its status, such as the repatriation of Native American objects

- Resolution of the disposition of an unclaimed loan

- Irreversible deterioration, or deterioration beyond the usefulness of an object (e.g., the self-destruction of a nineteenth-century, prevulcanized rubber shoe)

- Necessary conservation costs exceeding the replacement value

- Authenticity/attribution of the object found to be fraudulent

02-008: Refrigerated and humidity-controlled fur storage interior. Stephens College Costume Museum & Research Library. Photograph by Louise Coffey-Webb, with permission.

- Inability to care properly for the object (for example, cold storage for fur coats)

The American Alliance of Museums' (formerly the American Association of Museums) Code of Ethics (adopted 1991, amended 2000) requests that museums ensure that, among other things,

> disposal of collections through sale, trade, or research activities is solely for the advancement of the museum's mission. Proceeds from the sale of nonliving collections are to be used consistent with the established standards of the museum's discipline, *but in no event shall they be used for anything other*

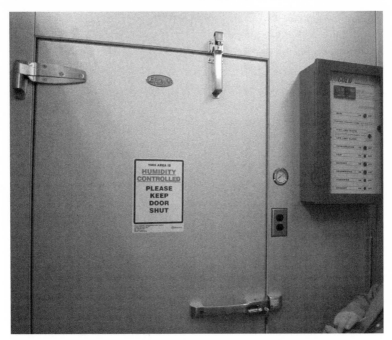

02-009: Refrigerated and humidity-controlled fur storage exterior. Stephens College Costume Museum & Research Library. Photograph by Louise Coffey-Webb, with permission.

than acquisition or direct care of collection.

It is irresponsible for . . . a tax-exempt institution to expend limited funds and space to store, insure, manage and conserve items of limited or no use to the Society or its goals. The American Association of Museums has a written Code of Ethics which provides guidelines for the removal of objects from museum collections. . . . When appropriate, items are placed with another museum or educational institution. The primary objective of de-accessioning is the improvement of the collection, not the generation of funds. If sale is necessary,

all funds generated are used to upgrade the collection either
by purchase of additional material or conservation of exist-
ing pieces. In this way, the collection can continue to grow
in quality and condition. ("The Sale of Deaccessioned Museum Objects: Why?" San Diego Historical Society newsletter,
September/October 1989 [emphasis added])

Once the governing bodies determine that an object is to be deaccessioned, some institutions require that the original donor/lender
be contacted, or at least a good-faith contact is made to apprise them
of the recent disposition of the object. Laws in California, Oregon,
and Utah bar lenders from recovering property loaned to a museum
after twenty-five years have passed since the date of the last written
contact.

The International Council of Museums (ICOM) code used to ad-
vise that proceeds from deaccessioning must go back into acquisitions, and did not allow even for conservation as an alternative direction for funds raised. More recently, however, the New York State
Museum, for example, has a slightly broader rule with regard to deaccessioning:

V. Deaccession

G. Proceeds derived from the deaccessioning of any property from the collection of the Corporation shall be placed
either in a temporarily restricted fund to be used only for the
acquisition, preservation, protection or care of collections, or
in a permanently restricted fund, the earnings of which shall
be used only for the acquisition, preservation, protection or
care of collections. In no event shall proceeds be used for
operation expenses or for any purpose other than acquisition, preservation, protection or care of collections. (New

York State Museum, "CHARTERING: A Sample Collections
Management Policy," http://www.nysm.nysed.gov/services/
charter/additionaldoc/collections.html)

Certainly, in the twenty-first century, the use of funds derived
from deaccessioning for continued care of the collection is quite acceptable, although using the funds for general operating budgets is
clearly considered unethical by professional associations. Often objects are transferred to other educational institutions. In this way, the
institutions are maintaining the original spirit in which the object
was donated, that is, in the public trust. According to the College Art
Association and the New York State Association of Museums, deaccessioned donations should find homes in other institutions where
they may continue to serve the original purpose of the donation.

Sometimes deaccessioned objects are auctioned formally in a suit-
ably distant part of the country. The suitability can be determined by
market or the public relations profile impact. Occasionally an object
will be placed on long-term loan to another institution where it can
be better appreciated and preserved. Auctioning does not guarantee
continual public access to a material resource. Consider the story of a
deaccessioned Galanos gown, purchased by an individual, then tak-
en apart and used to cover his car seats. If your institution is not in
a position to simply donate to another institution, perhaps you can
negotiate an exchange with another institution.

People making the deaccession decisions should be familiar with
the entire collection and knowledgeable about the objects. There have
been horror stories about eighteenth-century shoes (in poor condition) thrown in the wastebasket simply because they looked tatty
compared with more recent footwear to someone who was not familiar with historical footwear. Moreover, why throw out a beautiful
shoe because there was only one extant? There have been gorgeous

exhibitions of single shoes, and one shoe can tell us so much, if there is nothing comparable in the collection.

Deaccessioning a number of objects may appear to be a money-saver, as a by-product of creating a better storage environment for the remaining objects, or by allowing more care and attention to be spent on the remaining objects. For a public institution, however, detailed records, research, and contacting will need to be undertaken, and all this takes time. Time costs money. Also, if you do not want any evidence of an object once belonging to a museum collection, be sure to budget time to remove every labeling device from each object. Remember that another method of preserving storage space is occasionally to place a moratorium on collecting.

Be sure to update your inventory, location, and insurance records at the time of deaccession. It is advisable to keep all records, even the outdated ones, in case there are any questions down the line. If you do not already have a photograph of the object, be sure and take one at this point.

Finally, the obvious lesson to be learned from the deaccessioning experience is to try to prevent that necessity by being clear about your collection policy and mission statement, and scrutinizing every potential donation.

Chapter 3
Controlling the Environment

First Aid for Collections

Controlling your storage, gallery, or display environment will aid in the longevity and inherent value of your collections. "First aid" in this section refers to an immediate remedy, rather than in-depth treatment. Most costume collections are lucky to have a designated collection manager, and even fewer have access to trained textile conservators. Cost effectiveness does not encourage conservator services for rental collections, and indeed, the needs of rental collections often require restoration rather than conservators (see Glossary for the definitions of each term). Much can be done without hiring such a professional. However, the sad truth is that it usually takes a danger signal to provoke a need for change, along with the realization that some storage leaves much to be desired. For example, the roof of the attic where you normally store your hat collection begins to leak during rainstorms, or the basement where you store uniforms floods due to a burst boiler pipe. Or perhaps it is time to redecorate a display area and remove the framed objects, and their vacated space shows that a lot of fading has taken place while the objects were on the wall.

The vigilant approach known as *preventive conservation* is well worth every minute invested. While time seems an impossibly short commodity in the care of costumes, scheduling time for necessary preventive housekeeping is imperative to ensure the longevity of your collection. The design and setup of your work and storage space can also significantly aid your preventive measures. For example, rather than a speckled or mottled flooring to hide the dirt, insist on a white or light gray covering that will show the dirt plus any fallen buttons or pins. Be sure you have plenty of surface space for laying out objects and materials or tools—enough space to prevent compromising the space of one or the other. The need for sufficient surface space is frequently overlooked or not fully understood by those not actually engaged with the objects, but crucial to safe use of the collection. Designers of storage spaces may need to be enlightened as to this requirement. Access to storage, objects, and tools needs to be as easy as possible. This prevents, for example, dragging step stools around or other makeshift ways of extending your reach that could result in endangering artifacts around you. One useful tool to facilitate viewing of objects with reduced handling is to place them on a similarly sized piece of museum board on your worktable. This way, you can move the board around without touching the objects.

All these prevention projects may seem daunting. The best advice is to break up large projects into smaller parts, so that you can experience progressive accomplishments and be encouraged to continue. Do take the time to prioritize. Any time spent planning before doing is never wasted. Deadlines and projects can and do change daily, and decisions need to be made as to which projects only a manager or expert can truly do, what can be delegated, and whether it is safe, legally responsible, or even ethical to delegate certain projects, for example, to a volunteer.

Basic Preservation Techniques

Causes of Deterioration

Begin by identifying the effectors of deterioration pertinent to your collection, and be aware that many of these are invisible to the naked eye. The American Institute for Conservation (AIC) has identified nine potential agents of deterioration:

1. Direct physical factors
2. Thieves, vandals, and displacement
3. Fire
4. Water
5. Pests
6. Contaminants (pollution, molds, etc.)
7. Radiation (light)
8. Incorrect temperature
9. Incorrect relative humidity

Please also note the following additions to the AIC's list:

10. Abrasion
11. Additives to textiles, such as metallic salts, arsenic, and formaldehyde finishes
12. Chemical effects, such as oxidation, celluloid buttons deteriorating into nitric acid, reactions of dye chemicals, and proteins in silk tarnishing adjacent silver (see Figure 03-001)
13. Inherent fiber deterioration
14. Time

What You Can Do to Help

Many of the deterioration factors can be reduced with a monthly program of preventive housekeeping. Here are some suggestions:

1. *Light.* Keep unfiltered light to a minimum. Light damage is cumulative, and when the bonds of molecules are broken down, there is no repair. Fifty lux or five to eight foot-candles are the desired light levels. Incandescent lights are being phased out due to energy concerns, which is good news as they are known to generate heat. However, fluorescent lights are usually high in their ultraviolet

03-001: Celluloid button (1940s coat) with chemical deterioration in the form of crystals. Private collection. Photograph by Louise Coffey-Webb, with permission.

(UV) output, so it is necessary to add UV filters, which can be purchased from many archival supply companies. The filter sleeves can be cut to fit the traditionally long, tubelike bulb length. LED lamps are highly efficient, but at the time of writing have probably not been developed to their full potential as they are relatively expensive and tend to produce intense brightness in a focused direction. A motion-activated light system is extremely effective. Consultation with a lighting specialist is advised.

2. *Particulate matter.* Keep dust and visitors to a minimum. Your stored collection should not be viewed as a peep show for the public at large, but should remain accessible to workers, serious stu-

dents, and researchers. All visitors bring in invisible particles. Dust
can introduce many small creatures invisible to the naked eye (especially to the aging naked eye) that become fodder for tiny insects
that in turn are attractive to slightly larger creatures, resulting in
larger damage. It is best to use a high-efficiency particulate arresting
(HEPA) vacuum cleaner. Establish a regularly scheduled cleaning
and vacuuming plan. Have a HEPA cordless Dustbuster-style
vacuum in easy reach. Untreated and thoroughly washed muslin
and Tyvek make good protective dust barriers.

3. *Temperature and humidity.* Maintain a nonfluctuating temperature—60 to 75°F (16 to 24°C)—and relative humidity level (30 to 60
   percent relative humidity [RH]). It is more important to keep the
   environment as stable as possible rather than trying desperately to
   maintain the ideal recommended levels. The International Council
   of Museums' Costume Committee has published a condensed book
   of guidelines and recommends a temperature of 18°C (approximately 65°F) and RH of 50 to 55 percent. Their booklet is practical
   for the nonspecialist.

4. *Archival materials.* Use pH-neutral materials to protect and support. Create barriers whenever necessary out of Tyvek or untreated
   and thoroughly washed muslin. Recycled plain white bedsheets
   (usually poly-cotton) are fine draped over racks or shelves, as long
   as you wash them in very hot water and do not put any additives
   in the wash or dryer. In *Your Vintage Keepsakes*, Margaret Ordoñez
   describes how to make and shape padded hangers for premium
   support. "Sausages" have become a staple in most costume collections. Made of rolled inert polyester batting, then covered with
   muslin and hand-stitched closed, they work beautifully as form
   supports for folds in fabric, boots, hats, and so forth.

5. *Handling.* To avoid abrasion, the opportunity to snag fibers, and the

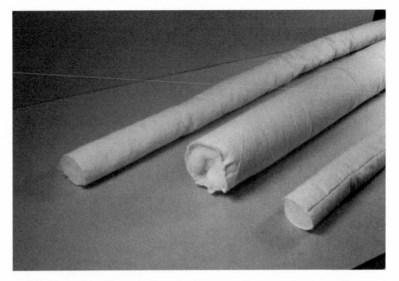

03-002: Examples of "sausages" made of ecru muslin over polyester needle-punched batting. Photograph by Louise Coffey-Webb, with permission.

transference of sweat or stains, keep handling to a minimum. Here are a few reminders:

- Have racks, trays, and workspaces, and inert sheets or tissue available when examining objects or pulling your collection.
- Have padded hangers, supports, and barriers prepared and at hand.
- Use a piece of museum board or even a few sheets of archival tissue as a tray on which to place the object on the worktable to move it around easily.
- Have photographs affixed to the outsides of boxes where possible.
- Obtain as much information in advance from your visitors or researchers, so that you are not pulling items unnecessarily.
- Wear white gloves when appropriate (see below).

- Wash hands before and after, even when using gloves.

- Remove dangling necklaces, bracelets, earrings, and protuberant rings.

- Hold the hanging garment by the hook of the hanger rather than the shoulders of the garment.

- Support the dress, if long, using the "fainting lady" technique: one hand holds the hook and the other supports the weight at around hip level.

- Always think before moving an object. Make sure there is a clean, unobstructed surface ready before you move it.

The use of white gloves while handling has its pros and cons. There is definitely something to be said for the cautionary effect of having a box of clean white gloves on the worktable. However, you are urged to consider each item individually as to the appropriateness of covering your hand with something that can reduce your own sensitivity to touch and can pick up dirt and transfer it easily. You may prefer plain washed hands, which are certainly preferable to putting on already-used and grimy gloves. It is extraordinary how quickly a white glove can get dirty. The lack of sensitivity may lead to slippage, too. Many people are now turning to disposable nitrile gloves. These are preferable in one way as they stretch and are very close fitting, resulting in greater sensitivity, which is important when handling delicate fabrics, laces, or complicated closures such as hooks and eyes. The synthetic rubber nitrile glove is also preferable to natural rubber latex, as many people are allergic to latex.

A Word about Fabric Care

This subject is almost as extensive as the number of different fabrics and fibers that exist in collections. The correct approach to under-

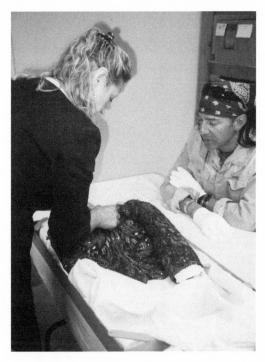

03-003: John Galliano and author, not wearing gloves in order to unhook closures with dexterity. Image courtesy the FIDM Museum at the Fashion Institute of Design & Merchandising, Los Angeles.

standing best-practice treatment requires knowledge of chemistry and textile conservation concerns and skills. For these reasons, the present volume does not cover this topic. In the meantime, do learn all that you can about different textiles, whether man-, animal-, or plant-made. Examine the construction of clothing and generally observe how garments are put together. Remember that museums generally have the word "preserve" in their mission statements, which means that they cannot perform restoration (as opposed to conservation) with a clean conscience. If you have a rental, study, or private collection, you may not be bound by such rules and therefore be open to a broader range of treatments. Whatever you decide to do, make sure you take before and after photographs and have all your treatment proposals in writing. The Smithsonian Institute and the American Institute for Conservation offer tips on choosing textile conservators.

Space Concerns

"Nature abhors a vacuum" is a phrase attributed to Aristotle. "Horror vacui" actually referred to the laws of physics. The phrase is also used in art composition, and here it relates to the inevitable quandary that storage and work space both seem to fill up effortlessly.

One of the most pressing concerns for collections is having enough space for correct storage. Running out of space happens to the best of us, even when we plan against it.

When costume collections are properly housed, they can take up to three times more space than they originally did. If you are looking at a collection hanging on conventional commercial plastic or even wire hangers, just imagine how much more volume the collection will take up on the hanging rod when you are using padded hangers. Add to that a muslin garment bag or two to provide barriers for the delicate or embroidered garments, and perhaps a second pants hanger to help carry the weight of a skirt train, and you will begin to have an idea of how much more space you may require.

Space concerns affect preparations for research and assembling objects for exhibition or other projects. Make it a rule to clear space before you begin a project. Have archival trays and boards at the ready. Remember to create a temporary or intermediary hanging space: If you have been asked to pull out a range of early-twentieth-century dresses, where are you going to put those you have already found while you continue looking for others? One suggestion is to have a couple of hooks on the ends of your storage areas or closets. Another is to use a rolling garment rack. Always put things away after use and attach reminder notes wherever necessary. Do not rely on your memory only!

03-004: Rolling clothing rack with canvas covers. Bonnie Cashin Collection of Fashion, Theater and Film Costume Design (Collection 440.) UCLA Library Special Collections, Charles E. Young Research Library, UCLA. Photograph by Louise Coffey-Webb, with permission.

Bearing all these challenges in mind, if you find yourself planning for a newly built storage environment, or you are the recipient of a convertible space, do be bold and consider doubling or even tripling your current storage requirements. It is a travesty indeed when collectors and collections are forced to deaccession holdings merely due to space volume demands, rather than any intellectual consideration.

A number of collections have been kept largely on industrial-strength rolling racks, as this was considered convenient for access in a crunched space—which it was. Not taken into account was the abrasion caused by moving the racks back and forth. Even if the person moving the rack was very careful not to brush against the next

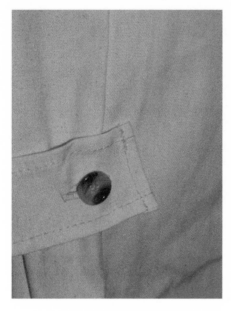

03-005: Detail of canvas tiebacks showing method of closure to be a button. Bonnie Cashin Collection of Fashion, Theater and Film Costume Design (Collection 440). UCLA Library Special Collections, Charles E. Young Research Library, UCLA. Photograph by Louise Coffey-Webb, with permission.

rack, the vibration within the rack will prove detrimental over time, and the swinging motion that sometimes happens puts added strain on the shoulders or straps. For ease of access, the garments in Figure 03-004 are stored on rolling racks with commercially available canvas dust covers. If you make your own covers from unbleached and un-sized muslin, you can avoid the problem of off-gassing that frequently comes with commercially available materials. Some closures are made with buttons, some with Velcro, and some with magnets (see Figure 03-006). Velcro is extremely handy, but beware the use of the "male" side of the tape with all its tiny loops if you plan to use it to close textiles other than those you are joining together.

Hanging versus Boxing versus Rolling
When is it better to hang, box, or roll a garment? The answer is

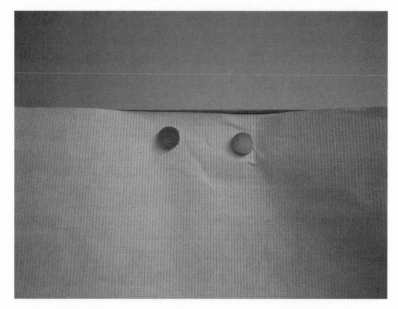

03-006: Magnets holding Tyvek dust covers to the metal storage container, American Textile History Museum. Photograph by Louise Coffey-Webb, with permission.

item-specific, depending on its delicacy and structure, as well as the tools and space available. Essentially, hanging garments are more accessible (see Figure 01-005). They can be seen instantly, rather than being unrolled or unfolded and removed from a box. A number of Eastern garments are simply rectangular (such as saris and sarongs) or structured with perpendicular lines (such as kimonos; see Figure 03-007), and therefore lend themselves to rolling—in the case of unstructured garments—or folding along the seams, but not hanging on a curved hanger. The same is true for many traditional South American garments, where adapted hangers work well only if they are strictly horizontal and wide enough to support the width of the cloth.

Hanging garments often require custom hangers, although archi-

03-007: Kimono "envelope" for storing folded kimono, with see-through window. Private collection. Photograph by Louise Coffey-Webb, with permission.

val hangers can be purchased. One advantage to using wooden hangers is that their arms can be sawn off to create a narrower shoulder. Once padded with needle-punched archival batting and covered with unbleached muslin, these work well. Be sure that the hook of the hanger is long enough for high collars. Sometimes the use of a second hanger, in the form of a suspended roll, works well to support the long train of a skirt. The first consideration is whether a hanger can sufficiently support the garment's weight. In many instances, a fully beaded garment (especially if beaded onto silk chiffon, as many 1920s garments were) will be too heavy to hang. Surviving nineteenth-century blouses may have extremely narrow shoulders and would

03-008: Hanging huipiles.
Mathers Museum of
World Cultures, Indiana
University. Photograph by
Louise Coffey-Webb, with
permission.

need to be hung on custom-width hangers. Using hangers that are too wide at the shoulder weakens the shoulder seam over time and causes splitting of the fabric. On the other hand, wide-shouldered garments from the 1980s require sufficiently wide hangers to prevent misshaping. Some skirts may be too heavy to hang, even if they possess additional waist strings. Sometimes when those strings are used, the uneven weight misshapes the skirt.

At many institutions, including the Kent State University Museum, hanging storage utilizing Venetian blinds (see Figure 03-009) was considered top-of-the-line in the late twentieth century. Blinds allow for airflow and can be adjusted to allow either for viewing or shutting

03-009: Hanging storage.
Photograph by Sara Hume.
Courtesy of the Kent State
University Museum.

out the light. However, occasionally the blinds catch a hanging tag or
sleeve cuff, which of course should be avoided, and for this reason
they are no longer considered ideal. Consequently many institutions
are now changing them for alternative barriers. In addition, there is
the perennial question of how to clean the blind blades.

Rolling a garment can be an excellent storage mode, if the tube
upon which you are rolling is wide enough, inert and ideally supported from within (see Figures 03-010 and 03-011). Velvet could easily
be crushed if not on the appropriate velvet roll (such as those found in
high-end fabric stores), and some items could be compromised if they
are lined, for example, and the lining is tighter than the fabric proper,

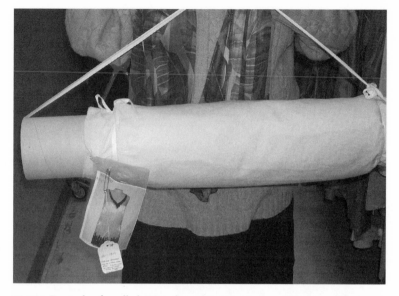

03-010: Example of a rolled 1920s dress. Western Costume Company. Photograph by Louise Coffey-Webb, with permission.

or vice versa. Boxing can be a very good method, *if* the garment is folded appropriately, by respecting the construction lines, and supported strategically, with ample space to accommodate the volume. Do not forget to interleave with tissue to prevent abrasion of the textile upon itself when rolling.

You might assume that hankies can be folded and put in a drawer or box, but if you were to prepare for the long term, you might follow the American Textile History Museum's lead by rolling them, as shown in Figure 03-011.

For premium storage conditions, even with lignin-free boxes, the archival tissue needs to be changed every five or so years. And however pristine the materials, a barrier of archival material must be placed as a lining in the box. There is absolutely nothing wrong with

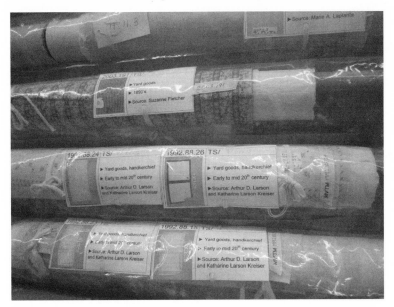

03-011: Rolled handkerchiefs. American Textile History Museum. Photograph by Louise Coffey-Webb, with permission.

lining your boxes with cotton or poly/cotton sheeting (preferably white) that has been washed and dried with no additives. These can be found at thrift shops for very little cost.

Deciding who will have access to your collection and how frequently will influence the design of your storage space, as discussed in chapter 1. Careful consideration needs to be given to the function of your collection, as well as maintaining the integrity of the objects, while allowing for optimal preservation. Compromises may need to be made, and inevitably you will settle somewhere along the continuum of the range of best practices. Many collections suffer from poor storage space, but it is heartening to see how creatively people make the best of their situations, as illustrated in Figures 03-014 and 03-015.

03-012: Flat storage (drawer) for 1920s dress. American Textile History Museum. Photograph by Louise Coffey-Webb, with permission.

Disaster Plans and Prevention

Security and Theft

There are various means to improve the security of your collection, such as locks on doors, screwed-down covers on display cases, and so on. Restricted access is most useful, as long as it is not totally inconvenient. When removing an object from display, always leave a note in its place stating (1) what the object is; (2) the date when it was removed; (3) the reason it was removed (e.g., for photography, a loan, or conservation); and (4) the approximate date of return. Imagine the surprise when seeing a note that simply states, "Object taken" (as has occurred), a note that might as well have been left by a burglar. If you have a security or janitorial service, they need to be alerted to read

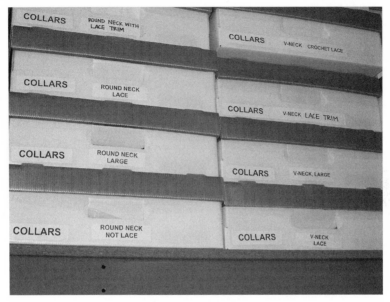

03-013: Examples of polypropylene boxes for collar storage. Western Costume Company. Photograph by Louise Coffey-Webb, with permission.

such notes and understand the message. Effective communication is always important.

When working at LACMA, I clearly remember being reprimanded by a guard for removing a prop earring that was about to fall off of a mannequin, even though I was obviously wearing my ID badge. Offended, I said that I was only doing my job, but I later realized that the guard was only doing his job, too. I should simply have explained to him in advance what I intended to do. That was a missed opportunity to communicate.

Basically, knowing where objects are supposed to be is a good preventive measure in itself.

If you have the budget, an electronic security system provides additional security. As with every other system, the procedures need to

03-014: Former work space in a closed-off stairwell. Woodbury University Fashion Study Collection. Photograph by Louise Coffey-Webb, with permission.

be maintained and crucial personnel kept apprised of processes and expectations. It is also a good idea to be friendly with your maintenance staff, as the following story illustrates.

When working with the Woodbury University collection, a professor came to work one day to find that one of the display mannequins in a locked case had a broken hand. How could this be? After checking with the maintenance department it was learned that the annual floor-cleaning event had taken place the previous evening, and it never occurred to anyone to alert the faculty. The display case is at floor level, and the cleaners had decided to move the entire case with the mannequin within, resulting in the dropped hand, then pushed the case back in place. Henceforth, an agreement was worked

03-015: Easy access to the collection at the Fashion Resource Center, School of the Art Institute of Chicago. Photograph by Jim Prinz, with permission.

out with the maintenance department that the professor should be notified before the annual floor cleaning, so that plans could be made at that time for any case moving or deinstallation.

Vigilance and communication are clearly essential tools for successful collection management.

Earthquake, Fire, and Flood

Different countries and even different states have varying legal requirements for safety and the protection of life. Publicly inhabited buildings—including museums, historical societies, educational institutions, and rental houses—need to adhere to certain codes, but you should also consider the objects for which you are guardian. For example, if your building has a sprinkler system, you may prefer to have an alternative fire retardant, since sprinklers may indeed put out

03-016: 1920s Jean Patou gown showing a water-damage mark at thigh level. Woodbury University Fashion Study Collection. Photograph by Louise Coffey-Webb, with permission.

the fire, but they may also render the collection worthless. Perhaps sprinklers may have been undeservedly maligned, as not all systems automatically engage in the entire building if there is a specific endangered area. Also, consider that however bad a soaked collection may be, the alternative is worse because fire completely destroys an object forever. I was involved with mitigating the damage to a large public institution's costume collection that was stored off-site. It was held in a building that was not specifically designed for artifact storage. When fires broke out in the area, parts of the collection were drenched by the sprinklers, and no on-site staff were immediately available. An interesting operation followed: Once the soaked items had been brought to the conservator's lab, and the registrar's office had performed its record-keeping duties, a search went out for electric fans and hair-dryers along with many extra hands from other departments. It was deemed necessary to dry the objects as soon as possible before too much bleeding or wicking of dyes occurred. Happily, many of the items were saved. Figure 03-016 shows a gorgeous gown that was acquired very inexpensively due to the water stain. The wonderful thing about many study collections is that they are being viewed for their inherent historic or construction components rather than their condition.

Disaster management is usually only an abstract idea, although the climate changes we have been experiencing in the twenty-first century will continue to cause disasters. It is always hard to truly imagine how we will act in disastrous situations, and however prepared we are, unforeseen situations inevitably occur. We are faced with learning from experience in spite of the fact that no disaster is likely to exactly repeat itself. One particular book has been very helpful in describing the process that unfolded during a real disaster: *The Fire at Uppark* (1990) by Adam Nicolson describes the events pursuant to a late-twentieth-century fire at a beautiful 1815 National Trust building in England, complete with lavish fully furnished interiors.

On the subject of fire suppression, Halon gas was considered a very effective system in the 1980s but has since lost favor. Halon is known to damage the earth's protective ozone layer. It is a compressed and liquefied gas that stops fire from spreading by halting combustion. Many Halon systems are still operational, however, and can legally continue to function using recycled Halon. Halon systems can be altered, but this book is not the place to cover the science involved. If you do inherit a Halon system, please consult a fire safety expert in your area for advice.

In the case of catastrophic disasters, all we can do is look back at Hurricane Katrina or Superstorm Sandy and try to learn from their losses and lessons. Today we hear about the cost of engaging the Army Corps of Engineers to bolster barriers to the water—expensive indeed, until we factor in the cost of not doing so. For this same reason we pay house and automobile insurance. Sometimes the prices seem astronomical, but if we went without, at the time of even a smallish disaster, our costs would be even higher.

Hurricane Katrina hit the Gulf of Mexico in August 2005, with devastating results for communities in Alabama, Louisiana, and Mississippi. Wayne Phillips, curator of the Costume and Textile Collection at the Louisiana State Museum, kindly shared some lessons he learned during that disaster. The institution already had a seventy-five-page disaster preparedness plan that was revised annually, and the entire staff was already on alert and well-briefed. Consequently, it took only eight to ten hours to secure the French Quarter museums by removing all the ground-floor displays. Some important recommendations were

- Designate a team captain for each building.

- Be sure to save the registrar's and director's office contents.

- Remember there will be no access to water or electricity.

- Be prepared to sleep in the museum/affected building.

- Have carts on wheels handy to move large objects, such as mannequins, away from windows, even if they are not on the ground floor. (During Hurricane Katrina, some windows blew in even when they when they were boarded up.)

- Always keep emergency supplies stocked and a camera handy.

If you are with a much smaller organization, you can take action on a lesser scale: besides having emergency supplies sequestered about your collection, house, and car, be sure to have charged flashlights, small fire extinguishers, and possibly a fireproof safe. When you buy yourself a new camera, keep the old one with your emergency supply kit.

In sum, the four basic stages of dealing with an emergency are as follows:

1. Prevention

Ask the relevant questions to obtain sufficient information to determine how to deal with an emergency.

Do a risk assessment of your vulnerabilities.

Get top management involved in the process (this is crucial).

Store duplicate collection records as well as emergency supplies off-site.

2. Preparedness

Be sure you have the support of management for your disaster preparedness plan.

Keep your plan alive by revisiting and reviewing it annually.

Make disaster-preparedness training part of your organization's culture.

Allow personnel to deal with inevitable personal issues first.

Prepare emotionally and take care of yourself.

Attend all disaster-preparedness workshops available and encourage sufficient preparatory drills.

Do not expect to use your institution, storage building, or warehouse as an evaluation site.

Remember that it is impossible to overprepare.

3. Response

Build a response team.

Know how to communicate effectively with your response coordinators.

Be prepared for disruption in communication services. (For example, during Hurricane Katrina cellphones were useless, but email worked. Even so, make sure you have a list of everyone's cellphone number, as well as alternate mobile communication devices, such as iPads or tablets.)

Be proactive and do not wait to be rescued.

4. Recovery

Control losses when failure occurs.

Locate insurance checklists.

Begin electronic data backup and restoration procedures.

There is some good news: In 2006 the Northeast Document Conservation Center and the Massachusetts Board of Library Commissioners announced a free online disaster-planning tool called dPlan (see www.dPlan.org). This excellent resource is specifically designed for nonprofit organizations and uses a fill-in-the-blank template as a basis for your own disaster plan. Smaller organizations are encouraged to begin with dPlan Lite, which has six main sections:

1. Institutional Information
2. Prevention (general facilities information and emergency shutoffs only)
3. Response and Recovery
4. Supplies and Services
5. Scope and Goals
6. Distribution/Review/Updating

03-017: Slide-out trays for specimens on type of crenellated rolling rack seen in cafeterias. Anonymous collection. Photograph by Louise Coffey-Webb, with permission.

Once you have registered with dPlan, you receive a reminder every six months to update your plan. This is a great tool for those short of time and staff. Do not feel badly if you do not already have a disaster plan; research conducted by Heritage Preservation and the Institute of Museum and Library Services (IMLS) has shown that up to 80 percent of institutions do not have emergency plans that include their collections.

The Getty Conservation Institute has published a guide for museums and other cultural institutions: *Building an Emergency Plan* by V. Dorge and S. L. Jones (1999). It is available for free as a PDF on their website. This publication is very thorough and assumes a large staff

03-018: Emergency supplies on rolling cart. Museum of Fine Arts, Boston. Photograph by Louise Coffey-Webb, with permission.

for its team-based approach to planning. There is a helpful disaster cause list, and while we all think of earthquakes, floods, and fires, we must not forget hurricanes, volcanoes, and acts of terrorism. The guide reminds us that treasures can be lost due to something as simple as a spent battery in a smoke alarm. If you have the space to do so, think about placing your emergency supplies on a rolling cart, as shown in Figure 03-018.

General housekeeping and vigilance are the foundations of disaster awareness, as well as pest awareness.

Integrated Pest Management (IPM)

IPM, as it is commonly referred to, is really a fancy name for good housekeeping. It recommends nontoxic prevention and the control of small creatures primarily by creating an unwelcome environment. Often very low-tech solutions are used, such as passive insect traps. The wisdom behind IPM is basically to break the food chain, primarily by maintaining a clean environment without using toxic substances, and by keeping a vigilant eye on intruders, with regularly recorded inspections that will help locate the main culprits. It is important to place pheromone traps at least fifteen feet from a doorway that is frequently opened. This is to prevent attracting insects from outside the doorway.

I was once involved as a consulting insurance adjuster for a dramatic moth infestation that, unfortunately, caused irreversible damage to the infested collection. The damage was considered irreversible due to the quantity of infested items, the extent of the infestation, and the future danger of infecting proximate collections. Cost was also a factor. The result was disposal of the entire collection. It had been stored off-site and had not been visited for months. Perhaps there was nothing troubling or visible to the naked eye upon the previous visit, but as usual, the phrase "just showing up" applies. If the premises had been inspected more frequently than every six months, the seriousness of the situation could possibly have been abated.

The Chicora Foundation in South Carolina is a nonprofit heritage preservation organization founded in 1983, specializing in programs and workshops throughout the southeastern United States. If you are not geographically close, the website provides access to inexpensive publications, such as *Managing Pests*, a twelve-page booklet, as well as a handy online newsletter, *Preservation Tips*. The Chicora Foundation recommends an IPM to instigate several procedures, such as the following:

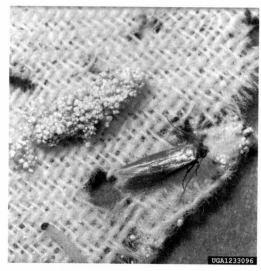

03-019: Webbing clothes moth (Tineola bisselliella). Life cycle. Photo by Clemson University— USDA CES, Bugwood. org, with permission.

→ Monitoring to identify the presence of pests

→ Understanding and recognizing the biology and life cycles of those pests

→ Strategizing and developing control measures

→ Continuing monitoring to evaluate those control measures

While Figures 03-019 and 03-020 show images of adult insects, note that most damage is caused by the larvae, with their voracious appetites for anything made of animal fibers. You can make many low-tech and hands-on procedures part of your IPM to deter insects. A few examples follow:

→ Make sure your doors have weather-stripping, sweeps, and thresholds (gaskets), and block all other small areas of possible insect entry.

03-020: Furniture carpet beetle (Anthrenus flavipes). Life cycle. Photo by Clemson University—USDA CES, Bugwood.org, with permission.

UGA1233095

- Remember to close all windows and attach fine mesh screens.

- Use artificial (silk) plants for display rather than live or dried plants.

- Vacuum frequently (preferably with a HEPA vacuum).

- Remove trash frequently.

- Eliminate moisture problems.

- Use insect deterrents or traps that are nontoxic and easy to check on. Pheromone traps use a form of "mating scent" in a tiny vial to attract moths, for example, to a suspended cardboard open box, in which a sticky substance is smeared to trap the insect.

- Do not be squeamish. If you see a moth, silverfish, or other insect, be prepared to squash it immediately, rather than let it get away.

At one institution where I worked, one of the storage areas was not far from the cafeteria. One morning there was a cocktail sausage that had been kicked under the door after a reception the evening before. Very soon thereafter, door gaskets were installed.

Apart from pheromone traps, commercially available moth repellents are highly effective, safe, and easy to use. For example, Moth-Away is a "green" moth preventative mainly comprising pyrethrins, which are nontoxic to humans and very distasteful to insects. These sachets can be found in housewares stores. Other possibilities include Eastern red cedar (Juniperis virginiana), lavender, lemongrass, peppermint, geranium, tansy, santolina, eucalyptus, and Southernwood (Artimesia abrotanum). Be advised that manufacturers may be reluctant to divulge their secret ingredients. It has long been known that the traditional mothballs our grandmothers used are very toxic as they contain paradichlorobenzene, and smell dreadful. If you receive a container with evidence of mothballs, wear a mask, remove the mothballs, and vacuum the objects thoroughly. In fact, an example such as this is one very good reason to separate new incoming objects safely until they are thoroughly inspected. If you are arranging or planning a new storage area, consider the addition of a holding area for just such a purpose. This is true for new donations as well as recently returned rentals. If you have ever been the victim of a moth infestation, you know how surreptitious and devastating they can be. Create a small supply box for your IPM, including traps, a flashlight, tweezers, small polyethylene ziplock bags, a magnifier, a small brush, insect identification references, pencils, and your pest logs. (See Appendix 2 for a sample pest management log.)

Online IPM courses are available, usually through conservation centers, such as the Northern States Conservation Center.

Other more expensive treatments include deoxygenation and freezing. Of the two, freezing is the more practical, although it requires stringent and knowledgeable approaches, so these are best handled through conservation labs and scientific entities. The Smithsonian Museum Conservation Institute has some good information resources online.

Insurance Issues

Perhaps the very first question to ask is whether your collection is covered by insurance. The building where it is housed may have some form of umbrella insurance, but is that enough? Adding an insurance rider to provide the policyholder with extra protection may be worthwhile. Ask your agent about coverage for your personal collection, because if it is not used commercially, you may have some coverage under your household or renter's policy. The business world has been slow in recognizing the value of antique or vintage clothing and textiles, but some definitions are commonly held: A *vintage* item is at least twenty-five years old, and an *antique* is at least one hundred years old. Anything less than twenty-five years old may be considered "used clothing" unless it is quantifiably collectable, that is, from a designer or of historical or situationally significant importance, such as having been worn by a celebrity. If you are part of an institution or organization, the registrar or other management office will be able to confirm the type of insurance you carry. If you volunteer for a nonprofit organization, both you and the artifacts on the premises should be covered; it is legally imperative for the organization to have such coverage.

There are three main types of insurance coverage:

1. *Property*, which includes the collection, furniture, fixtures, and so on.
2. *Business interruption*, which covers rent, salaries, utilities, and so forth, when the business is prevented from functioning.

3. *Liability,* which is coverage for negligence if someone trips, for example, or is injured by pins left in a garment.

You need to be conversant with insurance terms, so please discuss the following issues with your insurance broker or agent when purchasing your policy:

- Is the insurance coverage for cost or replacement value? Are you aware of the difference? (See the following section, "Appraisals and Valuation.")

- Can you insure individual items? How is this done? (This is usually the most expensive policy.)

- What does the agent think about being "coinsured," a term that refers to instances of sharing the risk and often reducing costs. In essence, you are implicitly agreeing to insure yourself.

- How does the state rate your insurance company? Some specialists believe that admitted versus nonadmitted status is not of critical importance. Generally, a company headquartered in the state where you are applying for insurance will have to comply with state law that may be more restrictive. The important matters are the company's financial rating and whether collecting from a smaller or offshore carrier will be difficult.

- Are security alarms required?

- What about the building's sprinkler system? You may be covered if the sprinkler system creates damage to your collection. Always ask your agent for conditions of coverage.

- Make sure you understand policy exclusions, such as earthquakes or flooding, which require additional coverage. Policy exclusions are contractual clauses that allow an insurance company not to pay on a claim.

+How will filing for a claim affect your policy rate upon renewal?

+Your business license may affect your coverage. In some cities an "antique" business license is preferable to a "secondhand" license, because "secondhand" can fall into the category of pawn shops, which are stringently regulated. The term *antique* usually requires that 90 percent of the merchandise or assets be at least fifty years old. When meeting with your insurance provider, bring your business license, tax statements, and other records that may be useful.

+When you are making decisions about insuring your collection, consider *how* and *if* you could recover from a disaster if your collection is destroyed.

+If you are researching insurance for the loan of artifacts or exhibitions, be sure to ask about offsite and in-transit coverage. It is common practice for borrowing institutions to insure the lenders' objects from "wall to wall"; however, be clear on understanding *which* walls.

Your collection can be insured without an itemized list, but in the event of a claim, accurate records are extremely helpful. An updated inventory that includes receipts, cancelled checks, pictures, condition reports, deeds of gift, records of restoration or conservation, shipping costs, and video records are all important in the event of a loss.

When insurance companies are regulated by the state insurance commission, their adjusters are licensed by the state, and their rules of conduct are regulated. If you have questions about how your claim is being handled, call your state insurance commission. Many states have public adjusters. These adjusters may rush to disaster sites and attempt to have you enlist their services to file your claim. Their rates are usually 8 to 15 percent of your total claim. They are knowledgeable about insurance claims but cannot take legal action if required. Be wary of public adjusters or lawyers who work on a contingency fee, and who push for a quick sell. For example, you may be advised to accept a fifty-thousand-dollar settlement when your loss is actually two hundred thousand dollars—a quick and easy profit for their negotiation. Plus it may be extremely difficult to get out of a contingency contract.

If another party's negligence causes your damage, that party may be covered by its own liability policy, and you may need to file a claim with your insurance carrier who will then *subrogate* against the responsible party.

Tips on Filing an Insurance Claim If Disaster Strikes

A real-life experience underlines the example described in this section.

An antique clothing and textile store was severely damaged by smoke and water from an arson fire next door. The firewall was compromised, white smoke filled the store, and flooding occurred from the huge quantity of water used to extinguish the fire. The proprietor learned the following about what a person should do in handling the long and involved claim process:

- Contact your insurance agent immediately about your loss.

- Take photographs or a video of the damage and start a journal with names, conversations, times, phone numbers and emails, actions taken, expenses, and observations.

- Be prepared to mitigate further damage, such as removing standing water and setting up fans for drying. Without electricity, you may need to rent generators.

- Isolate but do not dispose of items with mildew.

- Obtain (extra) rolling racks to move garments away from the areas of greatest damage. Racks can be moved around to help airflow and used again later for removing the collection if necessary. Rolling racks or rolling shelves can make instant compact storage as you move them to create various angles of access. There are plenty of commercial models available that go by various names, such as baker's racks or metro racks. You can place your storage boxes on these rather than stationary shelves.

- Be prepared to prove your loss to your insurance adjuster. For example, take photographs not only of your collection, where every textile touching the floor wicked water up three feet or more, but also of the wall where the watermarks were visible for five inches up the wall.

- A large dry-cleaning establishment, used to working with quality collections, was contacted to bid on moving and cleaning the inventory. The bid came in at approximately 50 percent of the entire property insurance, with a time frame of three to four months—besides which, the company stated that not everything could be cleaned and many items might be damaged during the process, so this was not a very desirable solution. Most facilities would not be able to handle a large volume (ten thousand pieces) without renting storage during the process, particularly when the garments are contaminated with smoke.

- It is necessary to obtain written bids for your adjuster.

- When the adjuster demanded an on-site inventory, the proprietor interviewed and approved of the professional art salvage company that would do the inventory. The cost was paid for by her insurance company, and she received a copy of the inventory and report.

- The adjuster insisted on ozoning—a process to eliminate smoke smell. This would certainly have been less expensive than cleaning. However, it is an extremely toxic process that does not actually remove the smoke particles and can cause long-term damage.

Fire, soot, and smoke damage pose special problems for textiles. It is always advisable to contact a conservator before handling a soot-damaged artifact. Handling can irreversibly drive sooty surface soiling deep into the fibers of a textile. The use of ozone to remove smoky and/or mold and mildew odors from a textile is not recommended as ozone will accelerate aging and degradation in many textile artifacts. ("Caring for Your Treasures," American Institute for Conservation Resource Center, www.conservation-us.org)

- Dry-cleaning and laundering may cause further damage, such as shrinkage, bleeding of unstable colors, or loss of information tags. And that is just the visible damage.

- There are so many variables in any insurance-related claim that it will serve you well to get advice from specialists and experts, such as credentialed textile conservators or people with years of experience in this area.

- Assess the damage and understand the cost or replacement value of your loss. If your records are sketchy, you may be able to get duplicate receipts from the original seller, or enlist an appraiser to help establish the value. Once you have provided the dollar amount for the claim, it will be difficult to amend it.

Four weeks after the fire, the adjuster agreed to pay for eight inventoried lots of the most visibly damaged items, but asked to have chemical tests on selected garments. After consulting with an attorney, the proprietor was advised that the insurance company could not physically do anything to her collection if she did not approve (such as chemical testing, moving, organizing, etc.). The insurance company does have the right to demand an expert opinion, however. Fortunately, the proprietor had not yet disposed of the most visibly damaged articles when their expert arrived.

The insurance company's expert was a licensed appraiser with an "interest in textiles" who observed samples from various parts of the collection. It still took several weeks to obtain a report. The proprietor then hired her own expert to evaluate the damage and write a report.

The landlord's insurance company informed the proprietor that she must move everything out so that building repairs could begin. Moving and storage companies pack everything in cardboard boxes, then seal the boxes in large wooden crates—a less than desirable situation for damp and smoky clothing. Public storage is generally not well lit or ventilated, and your insurance may not cover "new losses." The proprietor eventually found appropriate short-term rental offices. Ask real estate agents and colleagues for suggestions, as it is important to think through all the consequences.

When a major disaster strikes, contact experts or colleagues immediately. Professionals and specialists may be sympathetic and of great assistance, but they are often bombarded with requests for free advice. Please be courteous in this regard.

This proprietor had been in business for over twenty years and had never yet filed a claim. Insurance companies typically were granted huge rate hikes after the events of September 11, 2001. When it came time to renew at the new higher rates, she considered dropping the property insurance and only insuring for liability. This disaster occurred just five days before her policy expired.

Appraisals and Valuations

Let us begin by explaining the purpose, and therefore the necessity, of an appraisal. When a person wishes to give your institution a donation of her mother's mid-twentieth-century custom-made wedding dress, she may wish to take a tax deduction for its value. If she plans to take a deduction of more than five hundred dollars, she needs a professional appraisal. When you set up a business to sell used couture clothing, you will want to insure your merchandise. When a museum wishes to borrow your personal collection of nineteenth-century fans for an exhibition, the museum will ask for a valuation.

According to the Appraisers National Association, you may need an appraisal to

- Obtain specific insurance coverage.

- Claim an insurance loss on your [personal] property.

- Claim a loss for tax purposes.

- Itemize deductions for charitable contributions.

- Evaluate [personal] property prior to sale or other disposition.

- Know the value of your heirlooms or collections.

In this case, "personal property" refers to anything (e.g., furniture, jewelry, clothing) that is not real estate (real property).

Interestingly, as of this writing, there is no special qualification for evaluating costume and clothing. However, many associations bestow qualifications and proclamations with regard to appraisals, and most are concerned with real property (such as buildings) and fine art or jewelry.

The world of appraising in the United States has changed significantly since congressional authorization of the nonprofit Appraisal Foundation in 1987. The Uniform Standards of Professional Appraisal Practice (USPAP) were being created around the same time by a group of appraisal associations. USPAP was adopted by the Appraisal Foundation and has since become the widely accepted standard. For your collection you should find an appraiser who conforms to the accepted Ethics Rule presented in USPAP. Rather than cite the 119 line items in the USPAP publication of 2008–2009 regarding ethics, here is the essence:

- An appraiser must perform assignments with impartiality, objectivity, and independence, and without consideration of personal interests.

- It is unethical to accept a compensation arrangement for an assignment contingent upon (1) the reporting of a predetermined result, (2) a direction in assignment that favors the cause of the client, or (3) the attainment of a stipulated result.

So, in common language, do not hire someone who requests to be paid based on the value of the items, who is willing to take items in lieu of compensation, or who expresses an interest in buying one of the items in the appraisal.

As mentioned previously, there is no accepted standard for costume and clothing, so it is difficult to find such appraisers in this field who have sat through the hours of accreditation study largely aimed at real property appraisers. However, many associations throughout the nation have listings of appraisers.

In order to perform a professional appraisal, much time and research are required. Since an appraiser's costs may seem high in relation to the perceived value of the costume, you should help in whatever way you can. Make the garments easily available. Have photographs and all background details ready that could add to the appraiser's overall knowledge, such as provenance or related ephemera. In some cases, appraisers can work from afar if necessary, but they will need visual access to labels, linings, and so on to complete their work. You should also communicate to the appraiser the purpose of your request. For example, if you have a replacement value clause in your insurance, the amount will be what it would cost to replace the garment with one of similar and like quality within a limited period of time. On the other hand, fair market value (FMV) is the usual amount the garment would sell for on the open market between a willing buyer and a willing seller, with both having reasonable knowledge of the relevant facts. FMV is the method typically used for appraising donated garments. The final appraisal should have a cover document that states the intended purpose of the appraisal and the type of value sought, a description of the methodology used, an accurate description of the property items (one that could be identified without photographs, although today photographs are typically included), a statement of the appraiser's qualifications and impartiality, and finally, a signature.

Although the twenty-first century has seen an encouraging rise in the perceived value of used clothing of quality, the value, just as in automobiles, drops considerably the moment a new model leaves the showroom floor. For this reason, it is highly unlikely that a couture garment costing five thousand dollars when new would be worth anything near that a year later, unless it was owned by royalty or someone very famous.

With regard to donating a costume or a collection to a nonprofit institution, particularly if you wish to take a tax deduction for doing so, the IRS has a number of requirements. Rules and regulations continually change, so please research before making your decision by visiting the IRS website.

At the time of writing, the IRS form for Noncash Charitable Contributions is still Form 8283 and is required to be attached to your tax return if you claimed a total deduction of over five hundred dollars for all contributed property. If your nonprofit institution is receiving a donation valued at over five hundred dollars, you are required to sign the donee acknowledgment on this form (Part IV). According to the revised 2014 instructions, the donor will need to file an appraisal if a single clothing item is valued at more than five hundred dollars, and generally a noncash donation of over five thousand dollars requires an appraisal attached to the tax return. In the instructions for

Part III, Declaration of Appraiser, the qualifications for an appraiser are varied; in other words, as of this writing, there is no bottom-line license required, as is the case for real estate property appraisers. The Smithsonian Museum Conservation Institute has an excellent online resource specifically for textiles titled *Getting Estimates for Conservation, Repair, Insurance, and Appraisal.*

Consulting with your tax accountant is always recommended.

Chapter 4
Exhibitions and Display

Accessibility and Accommodating the Public

As the collection manager or steward of your collection, you will need to weigh the pros and cons of showing your collection. This step should be done when you create your mission statement and collection policy.

Museum professionals have long felt that exhibitions are the result of compromises between conservators and curators. Funding for cultural projects connected with clothing is at a worrisome low early in the twenty-first century. For that reason alone, you should be thinking of building awareness and outreach to the public. Admittedly, these actions may put the objects in danger of a reduced life span, but with no exposure of any kind, you could dangerously diminish available public and institutional support. Also, if decisions are made to sell a collection, there is no guarantee that items will be cared for in the future. As an example, some institutions sell their deaccessioned costume holdings at auction. This decision to deaccession parts of a collection in order to better care for the rest leaves one cold with the realization that something that was once preserved by a museum may now be lost for posterity, or at least for public access. Private collectors lend their objects to institutions for display or even traveling exhibitions, but usually at a great cost. These costs can include a rental fee, insurance and shipping fees, plus the cost of having a specialist provide descriptions and condition reports, custom-built shipping boxes or crates, travel fees for the lender to attend an opening party, and the guarantee that they will be able to keep the boxes and mounts at the end. It does seem ironic to forbid current generations from appreciating and learning from collections, and preserving them for the future, when we have no idea whether the collections will even be acknowledged in the future. Therefore, use objects today to inform and inspire current generations. In that way, the hope exists of a discerning future for them.

The question to be answered is how best to let your collection be seen while still preserving it. Much has been written about display techniques, and they vary enormously depending on budget and available labor. Margaret Ordoñez and Harold Mailand—in their respective publications, *Your Vintage Keepsake* and *Considerations for the Care of Textiles and Costumes*—address various tried-and-true techniques for mounting clothing and accessories and dressing mannequins. Karen Finch and Greta Putnam's book, *The Care and Preservation of Textiles*, also goes into some detail about mounting textiles, along with various Canadian Conservation Institute (CCI) Notes on the topic. Please refer to these volumes. Consider professionally mounting small, flat textiles as a means of combining both display ability and long-term storage. Some research collections have mounted their textile samples on muslin or wooden stretchers, either with one corner loose so that the reverse may be viewed, or a hole cut into the back of a mounted textile, in order to examine its reverse.

Some institutions have created permanent storage for flat textiles and quilts that is easily visible to the viewer with, for example, sliding storage panels or pull-out trays. In Figure 04-001, the quilts are resting on stretched fabric in aluminum frames, with roll-down dust covers secured by snaps and Velcro.

04-001: Pull-out tray storage for quilts suspended on stretched muslin. Photograph by Linda Baumgarten. The Colonial Williamsburg Foundation.

04-002: Open storage. T. B. Walker Foundation Textile Education Gallery at the De Young Museum. Image courtesy of the Fine Arts Museums of San Francisco.

Another popular technique is to build visible storage cabinets, or drawers deep enough to hold objects, that are secured with Plexiglas covers. This way, visitors can be walked through storage, be given a feast for their eyes, and you may not need to handle a single object.

Techniques and styles for open storage change with time, fashion, the latest preservation studies, and the availability of new materials.

The topic of mannequin dressing and display is vast and specialized, and suffers from fashionable changes just as much as clothing. Additionally, techniques and materials are constantly improving, frequently at the behest of conservators. The subject requires a separate publication.

Lending Your Collection

To lend or not to lend? There are numerous benefits to lending, although it is admittedly discomfiting to consider doing so. It need not be. The cost of shipping and insuring objects has become daunting lately, resulting in a strong trend at the beginning of the twenty-first century to lend less and less. Institutions are touting the display of their permanent collections as a kind of selling point. There are many benefits to lending, however:

- Disseminating information about your collection
- Increasing visibility for your work
- Increasing PR and recognition (particularly good if you are a charity or a business)
- Creating opportunities to receive feedback on your work
- Documenting public exposure, as required by many grant-giving entities
- Furthering your mission to educate and share

"Lending" a collection may also refer to the use of images of your collection and whether you have copyright ownership. Usually the institutional owner has copyright; however, there are instances when the institutional owner does not—for example, with some Erté or Marilyn Monroe images. A larger institution will almost certainly have a rights and reproductions department, and that would be the office to contact regarding an image, fees, and duplication rights. Institutions frequently allow scholars and serious researchers to photograph items in a collection if their use is for research rather than commercial purposes. If you intend to use an image for an educational presentation or lecture, please be collegial and credit the granting institution or collection from whence they came. If a publication follows, then it would be time to contact the rights and reproductions department.

However, if you are very short of staff and budget, you should weigh the pros and cons of lending. If another entity or institution has requested the loan, it is accepted practice to pass on the related costs, such as shipping, insurance, and even an administrative fee to cover the costs in time and labor of paperwork, phone calls, packing, and condition reporting. (See "Condition Reports" later in this chapter.) In these litigious days, both the lender and the lendee will probably have their own loan forms. If you are formulating your own form, be sure to include the following details:

- Duration of the loan.

- Value of the object.

- Who may handle the objects.

- Desired light levels.

- Whether the public may photograph the objects or whether they can do so only without using a flash.

- The level of protection—for example, must the object remain behind Plexiglas or glass?

- Temperature and humidity levels.

- Conditions under which the object can be used for publicity purposes.

- Who is paying for shipping costs?

- If a curator, conservator, or technical assistant needs to travel, who pays travel costs and per diem?

- Emergency contacts.

- Object's label copy and credit line.

- Pantone color book ID number for comparison before and after display.

- How the item is to be displayed, including method for securing to a stand, support, or mannequin—for example, where the twill tape or pins are attached, and whether mannequins need to have their stands screwed to a platform or wired like a tent rope.

Shipping, Customs, and Insurance

For many institutions, these functions are the domain of the registrar, but frequently the collection manager, guardian, keeper, or steward is the one to whom these responsibilities fall. In any event, there will be extra fees for insurance and for customs when shipping abroad. Some underwriters may request some form of proof of value, if insuring for a large sum. Many companies specialize in shipping, customs, and insurance, even in the specialized field of museums and exhibitors. Work with a local company where possible. On the national level, Fed-Ex has for some time offered White Glove Services featuring "specially trained drivers and specialty equipment for the safe transport of your most sensitive shipments," although I have no direct experience with these services. For details, see the FedEx website. Shipping overseas requires a Carnet, often referred to as ATA Carnet. It is an international customs and temporary export-import document that acts as a passport of goods. It permits duty-free export and import of goods, such as exhibition objects and display or mounting items. The Carnet is usually valid for six months to a year. There is an international Carnet system of which approximately eighty countries are members.

Condition Reports

It is difficult to summarize the issues that you may face with shipping; there could be many. Perhaps one of the more important safeguards is to have a record of the condition of the objects traveling before they leave home. These records, commonly referred to as condition reports, can then be compared to the actual condition of the object upon its arrival or just prior to being displayed. Condition reports should include

- A photograph or sketch of the object
- Description of all flaws before packing—for example, foxing (if a costume sketch, and notate where it is), missing buttons, stain at hem, ripped lace at sleeve cuff, or separation at seam—and the date of said description
- Description of treatment to be performed before packing
- Description of packing method to be used
- Pantone color number for comparison before and after display
- Space for the name of the person who fills out the form

When shipping overseas, remember that records of exactly the

04-003: Box for
eighteenth-century gown
with accessories, secured
with twill tape. Photo
© Museum Associates/
LACMA.

same quantity and quality that leave the country must be returned. Otherwise duties and penalties will be charged. Read up on the Endangered Species Act (often referred to as CITES) to see if your shipment contains any forbidden fauna, such as egret feathers adorning a hat. In one instance, a private collector lending to a costume exhibition in Japan took it upon himself to replace all the egret feathers with something similar, but unendangered, to avoid any customs problems.

Fashion shows, rental companies, and garment companies customarily ship their clothing on racks covered with industrial covers

04-004: Custom wooden shipping crate showing grid attachment to securely space hangers. Private collection. Anonymous photographer.

that zip entirely over the rack, and bars that clip all the hanger hooks in place. Rental companies typically ship garments packed densely and securely covered to avoid movement. Museums typically ship garments flat in boxes. There are many different methods for shipping costumes to avoid the garments slipping from side to side or up and down. One method is to attach a muslin "envelope" to a removable board inside the box and safety-pin it closed. Ethafoam spacers attached in the corners can help restrict internal movement.

In one unusual case, a bodice was so fragile that it was deemed too dangerous to keep taking it on and off the mannequin for each venue.

04-005: Wooden shipping tray with posts to support mannequin wigs. Photo © Museum Associates/LACMA.

Consequently it was shipped in situ on the upper torso, and a specially sized crate was made to accommodate it while on the mannequin. The reader may question why an institution would lend something so fragile. There are a couple of reasons. In this particular case, the garment was the centerpiece of the exhibition, appearing on all PR literature and the cover of the hardback catalogue. Also, when the loan agreement was made, the stability of the item was fair. It was only during the deinstallation process, before travel to the next venue, that the conservator decided it would be best for the object not to go through the dressing process again. Professional conservators and curators thus frequently find themselves in a position to reassess situations and make new determinations based on new criteria.

When I was traveling with a costume exhibition to Canada, the last venue, it was decided that some extremely large display props need not be returned. In order to comply with customs, an agent had to be appointed to come to the site and witness and record the destruction of said props before the shipping could proceed. It took quite a bit of extra time overall, and time can be an expensive commodity when working away from your base. But the time taken was weighed against the cost of shipping and storing those architectural props upon return.

Exhibition organizers or lenders occasionally demand that a project be bonded before it leaves the country. This is a form of insurance. It goes without saying that all expectations, let alone agreements, be in writing and signed off by both the lender and the borrower.

One last story: When I was hand-carrying Thomas Jefferson's actual clothing to Colonial Williamsburg for an authorized reproduction, two custom boxes were made specifically to fit the overhead compartments in the plane, so that I could be near them at all times. Needless to say, with two carry-on boxes, all my other luggage was checked. The Jefferson clothing arrived safely, but all my luggage and personal effects were lost!

Props for Display

As an exhibitor, museum, or historical society, when displaying your collection you are bound to enhance the artifacts or merchandise with supports, accessories, or other additional accoutrements, referred to as *props*. In some instances, these fans, mirrors, gloves, shawls, or buttons (just for example) may not necessarily be part of your historical or rental collection. While they should still be handled carefully, they are frequently more easily replaceable and not subject to the terms of accession or other such conditions. You may have more leeway, such as the ability to dye them, sew them, or even spray paint them. During one twentieth-century fashion designer exhibition, about sixty matching mannequins were used, with a plan to dress the feet in uniform women's pumps made of fabric. They were then dyed (hand-painted in some instances) to match closely the garments on the mannequins. Once used for the exhibition, the pumps were never accessioned into the collection.

If space is available, sometimes a good idea is to begin building a store of various props that can be used for displays. Thrift and charity shops can be useful resources for props, as items can be altered, trimmed, painted, and so on. Be sure to examine the items for insect infestation or mold. Shawls and fichus are useful for hiding insufficient back closures. Gloves may not fit the mannequin's hands, but can be artfully draped over a purse. You may decide to tag your props with a prop label so as not to face the worry, down the line, of someone spending time cataloguing and accessioning items never intended for long-term preservation. How do you differentiate between a prop and an artifact? This decision is subjective, based on the institution's collections policy as well as the exhibition style and practice. A prop is something that visually conveys an additional note of context, perhaps enhancing a silhouette, without detracting from the principal object on display. Often an accessory could be substandard, with its faults hidden or redressed, but the object, although sufficient as a prop, has been compromised and deemed unworthy of indefinite preservation in a museum or rental collection. A note of warning, though: There is never enough space to keep everything, and more often than not, prop items are rarely used a second or third time, with the exception of support petticoats and wigs that can be restyled.

The Angels Project

The Angels Project was originally conceived of and implemented by the American Institute for Conservation (AIC) in 1988. It was held in conjunction with the AIC's annual meetings, and its purpose was to provide expert assistance to local collections that did not normally have sufficient funding for conservators. In 2006 the Costume Society of America began its own Angels Project, headed by the team of Margaret Ordoñez (now-retired professor and director of the Historic Textile and Costume Collection, University of Rhode Island) and Martha Grimm (independent textile and costume conservator, Phoenix), and starting with the collection at the Connecticut Historical Society in Stonington. The Angels Project is a one-day event held each year in late spring, just before the annual Costume Society of America Symposium, and offers conservation, storage, and curatorial assistance to small collections in the vicinity of the symposium's location. The project is headed by textile conservators, particularly Martha Grimm, who forged a healthy alliance with the AIC. In recent years, the effort has been filmed and posted on YouTube. This is important work, and if you are managing a collection that might qualify for the Angels' assistance, you will find it an effort fully worth all the time you might put into preparing for this single day. You will be able to share previously unseen parts of your collection with a group of enthusiasts, certainly gaining valuable knowledge in the process. Your collection will be helped, not only in its conservation, but in its organization. See the Costume Society of America's website, www.costumesocietyamerica.com.

Summary and Your Checklist of Progress

At the outset of the twenty-first century, a wonderful publication was available titled *Benchmarks in Collection Care*, produced by experts all over the United Kingdom and published by the British Council for Museums, Archives, and Libraries. That particular council no longer exists, but there are still many online resources from Britain, which seems to be at the forefront of guarding and organizing collections and making that information publicly available. The work the experts did, including the creation of SPECTRUM (a standard for international collections information management), is now under the umbrella of the Collections Trust, based in England, but with international membership. The trust publishes professional standards that are being adhered to throughout Europe and which are pertinent to our efforts here. The trust's website offers a variety of museum collection forms and registers. The *Benchmarks* publication described three levels of collections care:

1. Basic practice
2. Good practice
3. Best practice

In terms of your own organizing work on your collection, any self-examination and consequent change management is a symbol of *basic* practice. Any improved awareness is practice. A *good* practice would be the implementation of improvements and systems that are practical for you and ethical for your functioning. The *best* practice would be similar to the preservation gold standard referred to at the beginning of this volume. In other words, the best that you can do with your given resources—as well as awareness and plans to raise your standards to a professional level, if not already met, including the notification of those decision-makers and purse-string holders who will help you to achieve the best practice.

Now is time to view your checklist of progress. How many of the following have you accomplished or begun to work on?

- Mission statement

- Collection policy

- Inventory

- Accession procedure

- Database

- Integrated pest management

- Insurance

- Disaster plan

- Collection procedures manual

Onward and upward!

Appendix 1
Useful Resources

Archival Storage Suppliers

Gaylord: 800.448.6160, www.gaylord.com.

Light Impressions: 800.975.6429, www.lightimpressionsdirect.com.

Metal Edge: 888.862.2228, www.hollingermetaledge.com.

University Products: 800.628.1912, www.archivalsuppliers.com.

Untreated Muslin

Fabric.com has 108-inch unbleached muslin, but it must be washed before using to remove sizing.

JoAnn Fabric and Craft Stores carry unbleached muslin; www.joann. com (and the same caution as above applies).

Testfabrics Inc., 415 Delaware Avenue, West Pittston, PA 18643; 570.603.0432; Fax: 570.603.0433; info@testfabricscom; www. testfabrics.com.

Needle-Punched Polyester Batting

Batt-Mart: 225 Mount Olive Road, Michie, TN 38357; 857.228.8464; www.batt-mart.com.

FiberCo Inc., PO Box 14728 (1300 Eden Drive); Fort Worth, TX 76117; fiberco@fiberco.com; www.fiberco.com.

Tyvek (Type 15442R)

DuPont, PO Box 80728, Wilmington, DE 19880-0728; 800.448.9835; tyvekinfo@dupont.com; www.dupont.com/.

FiberMark North America, 70 Front Street, West Springfield, MA 01089; 800.843.1243; Fax: 413.532.4810; www.fibermark.com.

Integrated Pest Management

Chicora Foundation Inc., PO Box 8664, Columbia, SC 29202; 803.787.6910; www.chicora.org.

Insects Limited Inc., 16950 Westfield Park Road, Westfield, IN 46074; 317.896.9300; Fax: 317.867.5757; www.insectslimited.com.

Master Herbalist Ltd. for moth herb sachets: Suffolk IP29 4EB England; www.themasterherbalist.co.uk.

Moth-Away manufacturer: Richards Homewares Inc., 3810 North Mississippi Avenue, Portland, OR 97227; richardshomewares.com

MothFree, 800.797.6747, www.mothfree.com.

Northern States Conservation Center online museum classes; www.museumclasses.org.

RugRemedyUK for a water-based spray moth killer: Woodcroft Farm, Water End Road, Potten End, Berkhamsted, HP4 2SH England; +44 (0)1442 866287; www.rugremedy.com.

Rack Dividers

Newhouse Specialist Company, 2681 Halladay Street, Santa Ana, CA 92705, 877.435.3859; sales@newhouseco.com.

Laundry Marker Pens

Retractable marking pens, www.staples.com and www.officesupplyinc.com.

Display Materials

Acrylic Glazing—Optium: Tru Vue Inc., 9400 West 55th Street, McCook, IL 60525; 800.621.8339; Fax: 708.485.5980; www.tru-vue.com.

General Information

Accessory custom storage mounts at the Museum of Fine Arts, Boston: www.mfa.org/collections/conservation/feature_costume accessories.

American Alliance of Museums (formerly the American Association of Museums), 2451 Crystal Drive, Ste. 1005, Arlington, VA 22202; 202.289.1818; www.aam-us.org.

American Association for State and Local History, 1717 Church Street, Nashville, TN 37203-2991; 615.320.3203; Fax: 615.327.9013; www.aaslh.org.

American Institute for Conservation, 202.452.9545; www.aic.stanford.edu.

International Council of Museums (ICOM) Costume Committee: network.icom.museum/costume/.

Canada Conservation Institute, 1030 Innes Road, Ottawa, Ontario K1A 0M5; 613.998.3721; Fax: 613.998.4721; www.cci-icc.gc.ca. The CCI publishes *CCI Notes*: "Intended for a broad audience, the Notes offer practical advice about issues and questions related to the care, handling, and storage of cultural objects. Many Notes are illustrated, and provide bibliographies as well as suggestions for contacting suppliers." Written by CCI staff, there are currently eighteen *Notes* pamphlets on textiles and fibers. www.cci-icc.gc.ca/publications/notes/index-eng.aspx.

Chicora Foundation Inc., PO Box 8664, Columbia, SC 29202; 803.787.6910; www.chicora.org.

CITES (Convention on International Trade in Endangered Species). Includes both flora and fauna; www.cites.org.

Collections Link! "Collections Link is packed with information, market intelligence, opinion and comment about issues that affect all those in the collections community in the UK and internationally." Managed by the Collections Trust, 22 Hills Road, Cambridge CB2 1JP, United Kingdom; www.collectionslink.org.uk/home/about-collections-link.

Color Association of the United States, www.colorassociation.com.

Costume Society of America, 390 Amwell Road, Suite 402, Hillsborough, NJ 00844; 800.CSA.9447 or 908.359.1471; national.office@costumesocietyamerica.com; www.costumesocietyamerica.com.

The Costume Society (UK),www.costumesociety.org.uk.

FedEx White Glove Services, www.fedex.com/us/services/white-glove/default.shtml.

Getty Institute, www.getty.edu.

Getty Vocabularies, http://www.getty.edu/research/tools/vocabularies.

Internal Revenue Service (IRS), www.irs.gov or www.irstaxforumsonline.com or www.irs.gov/taxtopics/tc506.html.

International Council of Museums' (ICOM) "Vocabulary of Basic Terms for Cataloguing Costume," available free from www.collectionstrust.org.uk; also linked from the ICOM website, www.costume-committee.org.

Museum Freecycle UK. Currently with over three hundred institutional members to offer online recycling of storage and exhibition materials, www.freecycle.org.

Northeast Document Conservation Center and the Massachusetts

Board of Library Commissioners' free online disaster-planning tool, dPlan, www.dPlan.org.

Northern States Conservation Center classes: www.museumclasses. org

Pantone, www.pantone.com.

Smithsonian Museums Conservation Institute, *Getting Estimates for Conservation, Repair, Insurance, and Appraisal,* specifically for textiles: www.si.edu/mci/english/learn_more/taking_care/texrep. html.

SPECTRUM, The UK Museum Documentation Standard. Managed by the Collections Trust, WC 209 Natural History Museum, Cromwell Road, London SW7 5BD, United Kingdom; www. collectionstrust.org.uk. Their SPECTRUM Advice Fact Sheets are most useful.

STASH, Storage Techniques for Art, Science and History, www. stashc.com. A website providing information, tools, and resources to help create safe and appropriate storage solutions.

Computer Database Resources

Canada Heritage Information Network (CHIN), www.pro.rcip-chin. gc.ca.

Costume Inventory. Available from Costume & Theatre Inventory Resources, 855.468.8247; www.costumeinventory.com.

Excel. The following website has information on Excel for Mac: www.office.microsoft.com/en-us/excel/.

FileMaker Pro. The following website has information on FileMaker Pro for PCs (Microsoft) and Macs: www.filemaker.com.

International Council of Museums' (ICOM) "Vocabulary of Basic Terms for Cataloguing Costume," available free from www.

collectionstrust.org.uk; also linked from the ICOM website, www.
costume-committee.org.

MCN (Museum Computer Network). "Helping information professionals use technology to serve their institutions"; www.mcn.edu.

Northeast Document Conservation Center and the Massachusetts
Board of Library Commissioners' free online disaster-planning
tool, dPlan, www.dPlan.org.

PastPerfect Museum Software—PastPerfect Software Inc., 300 North
Pottstown Pike, Suite 200, Exton, PA 19341; 800.562.6080; Fax:
610.363.7845; www.museumsoftware.com.

Rental Tracker Inc., 12481 Tejas Court, Rancho Cucamonga, CA
91739; 888.595.8041; www.rentaltracker.com. Costume program
with bar codes.

Willoughby Associates, Limited. The Museum Software People;
www.willo.com. (Willoughby Associates has recently been taken
over by Selago Design Inc.; http://www.selagodesign.com/.)

Appendix 2

Forms You Can Use

1. Storage Workbox List

2. Collection Handling Rules

3. Sample *Bento 4* sheet

4. Costume Piece Worksheet

5. Recommended Label Placement

6. Integrated Pest Management Log

Storage Workbox List

NB: A fishing tackle box is usually less expensive than an art supply box.
Archival labels
Basic sewing kit, including curved or upholstery needles and extra-fine
    or silk pins
Bulldog clips
Camera
Clean white cotton or nitrile (latex-free and powder-free) gloves
Compact multitools (e.g., Leatherman or small Swiss Army knife)
Emery boards (to file scratchy fingernails)
Laundry-marking pen (preferably retractable) for twill tape
    label-writing
Paperclips
Pencils
Post-Its
Q-tips or cotton ear buds
Safety pins (large and very small)
Tweezers
Twill tape
Vacuum, mini (computer keyboard) battery-powered
Ziplock polyethylene bags (large to very small—for collecting loose
    beads, etc.)

Other (too big for tackle box)

Archival tissue precut to smaller pieces
Batting (for shaping and supporting)
Clean rags
Dustbuster or similar small vacuum
Abaca fiber tissue
Mylar (sheets and envelopes)
Sheet protectors
Washed white sheets

Collection Handling Rules

1. Preparing Yourself

   Wash hands (and do not put on hand lotion).

   Wear gloves if required or when handling metals or coated fabrics (e.g., vinyl, lacquer, jewelry). If not wearing gloves, be sure your fingernails are filed smoothly.

   Remove all rough-edged, protruding, and dangling jewelry (e.g., rings, bracelets, earrings, necklaces). Wedding bands are acceptable if smooth.

   Do not cough, sneeze, or bleed onto the collection (turn away and use a tissue).

   Tie back long hair.

2. Preparing the Workspace

   Spread a clean sheet on the worktable.

   No food or drink in the workspace.

   No ink pens in workspace.

3. Handling the Costume

   Lift clothing off rack using hanger hook, not shoulder.

   Support weight of garment with other arm before placing on the table.

   Do not remove any tags (including hanging or sewn on).

   Use a "pick" or tweezers and Loupe magnifier to examine, rather than your finger.

   Photographs may be taken for research purposes only.

4. Finishing Up

   Before replacing garment on hanger, fasten all closures again.

   If in box, replace any padding or tissue.

   Report any loose components or evidence of insects or mold.

Please sign that you have read and will abide by these rules

Thank you for your consideration in prolonging the life of this collection.

Sample *Bento 4* Sheet

Coffey-Webb Private Collection

Object
Woman's Pajamas

Designer/Artist/Manufacturer
Bedhead, Los Angeles

Sequence Number
1

Medium and Color
Cotton print with pink piping and pink, green and mauve flowers

Description
Two piece pajama set for woman, of printed floral cotton.

Size (HxWxD)
small

Accession Number
2011.01A-B

Date of Object

Location
Storage Area 1 Bedroom

Accessories
none

Techniques
Polychrome print
Piping
Button and drawstring closure
Pocket and lapel

Image

Close-up

Extra Image files

Provenance
Made in Los Angeles, CA.
Purchased at "It's A Wrap" (clothing from TV/Film productions) on Magnolia Boulevard in Burbank, 2009.

Date of creation

	From:	To:
1	2005	2009

Buyer/Seller Info

Sample Costume Piece Worksheet from Costume & Theatre Inventory Resources

Date Entered in DB: [   ]

Costume Piece Worksheet

Photo File Name: [   ]

Tag ID: [   ]   Costume: [   ]

Costume Description: [   ]

Costume Type: [   ]   Color: [   ]   Group / Category: [   ]

Fabric: [   ]   Time Period: [   ]   Special Effects: [   ]

Adult / Child: [   ]   Size: [   ]   Gender: [M   F]

Costume Designer: [   ]   Source: [   ]   Date Acquired: [   ]

Total Cost To Make/Buy [   ]   Total Replacement Cost [   ]   OK To Loan / Rent? ☐ Rental Fee [   ]

Cleaning Code: [   ]

Storage Location: [   ]   Current Location: [   ]

Needs Repair ? ☐   Repair Description: [   ]

Chest: [   ]   Waist: [   ]   Hips: [   ]   Girth: [   ]   Neck: [   ]

Sleeves: [   ]   Neck-to-Waist: [   ]   Waist-to-Hem: [   ]   Inseam: [   ]

Notes: [   ]

This Costume Piece belongs to the following Ensemble:

[   ]

Costume Types:

Accessories	Belt	Bloomers	Blouse	Bodice
Bra	Breeches / Knickers	Cape	Coat	Collar / Jabbot
Crown / Tiara	Cuffs	Cumberbund	Dance Dress - leotard	Dress
Hat	Jacket	Leotard	Other	Panier / Bustle
Pants / Slacks	Robe	Romantic Tutu	Scarf	Shirt
Shoes	Skirt	Suit Jacket	Tie	Tights
Tutu	Unitard / Jumpsuit	Vest	Wig	

Colors

Color			
Black	Black / White Str	Blue	Brown
Clear / Transpar	Cream	Gold	Gray
Green	Orange	Pink	Purple
Red	Silver	Tan / Nude	White
Yellow			

Special Effects

Watercolor	Shredded
Old and Torn	Electric Lights

Cleaning Codes

1-Do Not Clean
2-Dry Clean Only
3-Gentle hand wash in cold water; use Woolite or similar mild detergent, rinse well and drip dry
4-Machine Wash OK
5-Hand wash in Wig Shampoo in luke warm water only. Hang upside down to dry.

Recommended Label Placement for Garments/Accessories

Hat/headdress: Inside crown where the crown and brim meet, center back.

Capes/cloaks: Inside neck opening on proper left side.

Garment with sleeves: Inside bottom of proper left sleeve at seam or lining.

Sleeveless garment with armhole: Inside proper left armhole at bottom of side seam.

Sleeveless garment without armhole: At center back or where garment fastens (and make sure label is not obscured between layers when buttons/hooks are fastened).

Pants/skirt: Inside at waist opening where garment fastens (and make sure label is not obscured between layers when buttons/hooks are fastened).

Gloves: Inside at underside of wrist at seam if possible, on proper left glove if differentiated.

Stockings/socks: Inside top of center back seam, on proper left stocking if differentiated.

Handbag/purse: Inside at side seam if possible or near manufacturer's label.

Flat accessory, e.g., shawl, handkerchief, scarf, or fichu: In a corner on the wrong side opposite the monogram/logo, or next to manufacturer's label, or center back for fichus and berthas.

(Based on Nancy Rexford's *Rules for Consistent Tag Placement*, circa 1985, with permission.)

Sample Pest Management Log

PEST MANAGEMENT LOG

Today's Date _____ Reporting Party _____

Gallery_____ Office_____Storage Area_____

Materials/Objects of Concern_____

OBSERVATIONS

Evidence: Frass ____ Larva ____ Pupa ____ Body Casings ____ Adult insect ____
(Life stage and quantity)

           Insect ID _____ Live_____ Dead _____

TREATMENT

Trap: No___Yes___   Type_____ Location_____ Date_____

Trap Replacement Date _____ Vacuum Date/s _____

Barrier *(Type/placement/date)* _____

Other Recommendations _____

Glossary

This glossary can help you communicate more effectively with registrars, shippers, insurers, appraisers, conservators, curators, and dealers.

abaca fiber tissue: A very fine and soft natural-fiber-based archival tissue, used for very delicate objects.

abrade: Scrape or wear away by rubbing.

accession: A formal acknowledgment of an object into a collection, with an official transfer of title and the designation of a unique identifying number. The object is accessioned before it is catalogued.

acquisition: The procurement of an object, before being accessioned. It may be donated, bequeathed, purchased, or exchanged.

acid-free: Inert. Often used in lieu of the term *archival.* Materials produced from any cellulose fiber with a pH of 7 or higher. (A pH of 7 is considered neutral, and below pH7 is acidic.) Acids weaken fibers and can change dyes. (*See* pH.)

appraiser: A person who is qualified to create a valuation for the pertinent property, executed for specific purposes following specified guidelines. A *certified appraiser* has been awarded this designation by a test and through the Appraisers Association of America or the American Society of Appraisers.

archival: A general term to imply pH neutrality or inert materials. A nontechnical term to suggest that a material or product is durable or chemically stable, and that it can therefore be used safely for preservation purposes. The phrase is not quantifiable; no standards exist that describe how long an "archival" or "archivally sound" material will last.

ATA Carnet: ATA is the acronym for "Admission Temporaire/Temporary Admission" combining both French and English. Carnet is an international customs document administered by the World Customs Organization (www.wcoomd.org) as well as the International Chamber of Commerce (www.iccwbo.org) used for importing and exporting goods duty-free, such as those in exhibitions, internationally.

barrier: An inert material used to protect an object from an external element, such as dust, not conducive to its preservation.

brisé: A type of fan with separate sticks joined by fabric.

buffered: Impregnation with a chemical (calcium carbonate) that maintains the pH level, but is particularly bad for wool and silk (proteinaceous fibers) and does not retain the preferred pH level for long. Basically to be avoided. Use unbuffered tissue instead.

catalogue (catalog): Verb and noun. Verb: the methodical act of classifying objects and describing them in a way that uniquely identifies them. Noun: (1) A compilation or publication listing all objects in an exhibition or a collection; or (2) for an individual object, a listing of its appearances in exhibitions or publications (cf. accessioning).

collection policy: A declaration of your collection's purpose, your audience, and your parameters for collecting.

condition report: Documentation, usually with measurements and images, to record the condition of an object at a given time. Conservators use procedures to record the condition of an object before, during, and after their treatment, and outline in detail treatment methods and materials used.

conservation: The science of preserving objects involving specialized education, technical skills, intellectual knowledge, and practical apprenticeship. In textile conservation today, the accepted practice is to perform work that can be removed or reversed without further deteriorating the object. The conservation profession is devoted to the preservation of cultural property for the future, and activities include examination, documentation (conservators do not perform accession), treatment, and preventive care, supported by research and education.

conservator: A professional whose primary occupation is the practice of conservation and who, through specialized education, knowledge, training, and experience, formulates and implements all the activities of conservation in accordance with an ethical code such as the AIC Code of Ethics and Guidelines for Practice. The conservator today has an undergraduate university degree as a minimum. The conservator preserves cultural heritage while retaining the integrity of the object, including its historical significance, context, and aesthetic aspects.

ephemera: Something that is created to exist for just a short time, such as event invitations, greeting cards, or theatre tickets.

Ethafoam: Polyethylene foam that holds its shape well but can be carved easily.

fair market value (FMV): The price that property would sell for on the open market between a willing buyer and a willing seller, with both having reasonable knowledge of the relevant facts.

ferrule: The top of a parasol or umbrella.

foxing: Stains, specks, and blotches in paper that are fungoid in nature and caused by relative humidity greater than 75 percent. The paper is usually acidic, though the growth of the fungus might contribute to that. It can also refer to tiny speckles on cotton and linen resulting from fine iron particles left as residue after washing in water with high iron content.

frass: Debris or excrement produced by insects.

HEPA: Acronym for high-efficiency particulate air, and usually used as a way of designating the effectiveness of filters for vacuums that can remove at least 99.97 percent of particulate matter, such as dust, pollen, mold, and bacteria.

inert: Chemically inactive.

IPM: Acronym for integrated pest management, which comprises good housekeeping, vigilant observation, and nontoxic insect infestation prevention.

LED: Light-emitting diode lamp. Energy-efficient lighting with high light output.

lignin: A component of the cell walls of plants that is a large, complex organic molecule that binds the cellulose together in a tree. It is largely responsible for the strength and rigidity of plants, but its presence in paper and board is believed to contribute to chemical deterioration, by breaking down to form acids and peroxides. It can be removed during manufacture. No standards exist for the term "lignin-free," and additional research is needed to determine the precise role of lignin in the durability and permanence of paper.

05-001: Early-twentieth-century cotton blouse showing lignin stain from wooden hanger. Anonymous collection. Anonymous photographer.

loupe: Manual magnifier that is small and powerful and good for looking at weave structure.

lux: Foot-candle. A unit of light intensity measurement, taking into account the area covered.

mannequin: A clothes form, usually with arms, head, and legs, used in displays.

mission statement: A declaration of your company's or organization's goals and purpose that guides your actions.

Munsell: A color system created by Professor Albert H. Munsell in the early twentieth century, based on analyzing three dimensions: hue, value, and chroma or saturation.

museum board: Archival corrugated board that can be cut to size. Often pale blue in color.

Mylar: A registered trademark for a DuPont material for a form of polyester resin used to make clear inert film.

off-gassing: The invisible emission of degrading gases. Woods and other materials give off organic acid vapors for years, and these gases deteriorate textiles, especially those with metals.

open storage: A term describing carefully designed storage cabinets that serve to show off their contents.

Pantone: A world-renowned authority on color and provider of color systems (name derives from the Greek *pan* meaning "all").

paradichlorobenzene: An odorous chemical compound that is highly toxic and used to make commercial mothballs.

pH: A measure of the concentration of hydrogen ions in a solution (the "H" stands for hydrogen, and the "p" is from the Greek *potens,* meaning "power"), which indicates acidity or alkalinity. The pH scale runs from 0 to 14, and each number indicates a tenfold increase. The goal is pH neutral: 7. Numbers above 7 indicate increasing alkalinity, with 14 being the most alkaline. A pH below 5 is considered highly acidic. Buffered storage materials typically have a pH between 7 and 9.

Plexiglas: Transparent acrylic resin sheeting used to replace glass.

polyester: The common name for the thermoplastic polyethylene tere-
phthalate, which is transparent with high tensile strength. It is also
chemically stable. Often referred to as Mylar. In England, polyethylene is known as polythene.

polyethylene: See polyester.

polyvinylchloride (PVC): A synthetic material that is quite sturdy but
unstable over time, and that off-gasses.

preservation: A broad term to encompass all preservation concepts, including artifacts, buildings, tribes, and landscapes. *Historic preservation* is frequently used in reference to buildings and cityscapes. The
primary goal of preservation is to prolong the existence of cultural
property through activities that minimize chemical and physical
deterioration and damage, and that prevent loss of informational
content.

preventative: A noun, as in the tool used for preventive action, such as in
inert barrier.

preventive: An adjective, as in *preventive care* or *preventive conservation.* The action taken to minimize further deterioration of cultural
property. The mitigation of deterioration and damage through the
stabilization of the environment surrounding an artifact, such as
appropriate handling and maintenance procedures for storage, exhibition, packing, transport, and use; integrated pest management; and
emergency preparedness and response.

primary source: Resource materials that are original or at least unfiltered
through time or translation in any form and more reliable for accuracy than secondary or tertiary sources.

prop: A term to denote a portable object or one of little or compromised
value, used to enhance a presentation.

proper left/right: Term used by museums and conservators to avoid confusion. The proper left is the left side if you were wearing the object

yourself, rather than your left as you look at the object (which would
be the proper right). Often written as PL.

provenance: A record of the history of ownership, place of origin, or
both.

public trust: The idea that resources or collections are to be available to
the public; often government-funded.

replacement value (RV): An insurance term meaning the amount it
would cost to replace an item with one of similar and like quality
purchased in the most appropriate marketplace within a limited amount of time. It is important to note that provenance is not
replaceable, that is, the replaced object, though it may be identical in
appearance, was not owned by the famous person with the historical
association of the original object.

restoration: Application of skills to enhance the aesthetic appearance
of an object or to return it to the look of its original state. Could
include redyeing, replacing, and other forms of reworking. Often
nonoriginal or modern materials are used, and practitioners do not
normally keep documentation of this process. An attempt to bring
cultural property closer to its appearance at a particular period of
time. Not to be confused with *conservation*, although international
travelers should note that terms are understood differently in different countries. For example, *conservateur* usually means "curator" in
French-speaking countries, while *restorateur* usually means "conservator."

RH: Abbreviation for *relative humidity*, the amount of moisture content
in the air compared to the amount of moisture the air is capable of
holding at a given temperature. The warmer the air, the greater the
amount of moisture content it can contain. The converse is true, too.

sheet protector: Top-loading clear covers for documents, usually eight
and a half by eleven inches with holes for a three-ring binder.

stabilize: Treating an object in a way that maintains its cultural integrity
but minimizes deterioration.

twill tape: White or ecru cotton or poly/cotton twill weave tape, approximately a half inch wide, frequently used for sewn-on labels.

Tyvek: A registered trademark for a DuPont material commercially
produced since 1967. Made from fine, high-density polyethylene
fibers randomly spun and bonded with heat and pressure to form
a remarkable fabric that is resistant to water, chemicals, punctures,
tears, and abrasion, while remaining vapor-permeable. It is also
washable and low-linting—in other words, a perfect material for
flexible barriers. Tyvek has become a fabric of choice for many textile conservators.

UV: Ultraviolet rays in visible light. More present in sunlight and
fluorescent light than in incandescent light. Potentially damaging to
fibers with irreversible effects because the damage is on a molecular
level.

Select Bibliography

American Alliance of Museums. "Debate over Deaccessioning." *MUSEUM News*, March/April 1990.

Armstrong, Jemi, and Linda Arroz. *A Guide to Buying and Collecting Affordable Couture*. London: Vivays Publishing, 2012.

Ashelford, Jane. *Care of Clothes*. London: National Trust, 1997.

Baca, Murtha, ed. *Introduction to Art Image Access: Issues, Tools, Standards, Strategies*. Los Angeles: Getty Information Institute, 2002. (The impetus for this book is the art information community's very real need for practical guidelines on how to lead end-users to relevant images of art and architecture online.)

Benchmarks in Collection Care for Museums, Archives and Libraries: A Self-Assessment Checklist. London: Council for Museums, Archives, and Libraries, 2002. (A 2011 edition was also published, but both are out of print.)

Besser, Howard. *Introduction to Imaging*. Rev. ed. Los Angeles: Getty Research Institute, 2003. (Designed to help curators, librarians, collection managers, administrators, scholars, and students better understand the basic technology and processes involved in building a deep and cohesive set of digital images and linking those images to the information required to access, preserve, and manage them. Excellent glossary.)

Bourcier, Paul, Ruby Rogers, et al. *Nomenclatures 3.0 for Museum Cataloging: Robert G. Chenhall's System for Classifying Man-Made Objects*. AltaMira Press, American Association for State and Local History, 2010. (PastPerfect Museum Software uses this lexicon.)

Case, Mary, ed. *Registrars on Record: Essays on Museum Collections Manage-*

ment. 3rd printing. Washington, DC: Registrars Committee, American Association of Museums, 1995 (1999).

Cumming, Valerie. *Understanding Fashion History*. Los Angeles: Quite Specific Media Group, 2004.

Defining the Conservator: Essential Competencies. Washington, DC: American Institute of Conservation, 2003.

Dorge, Valerie, and Sharon Jones, comps. *Building an Emergency Plan: A Guide for Museums and Other Cultural Institutions*. Los Angeles: Getty Conservation Institute, 1999.

Finch, Karen, and Greta Putnam. *The Care and Preservation of Textiles*. London: B. T. Batsford, 1985.

Hogue, Charles L. *Insects of the Los Angeles Basin*. Los Angeles: Natural History Museum of Los Angeles County, 1993.

ICOM. *Statutes: Code of Ethics for Museums*. Paris: International Council of Museums, 1987.

Internal Revenue Service. *Charitable Contributions: Substantiation and Disclosure Requirements*. Tax Exempt and Government Entities. Exempt Organizations. Publication 1771 (Rev. 9-2011). Catalog Number 20054Q. Washington, DC: Department of the Treasury.

Kelly, Kenneth L., and Deanne B. Judd. *Color: Universal Language and Dictionary of Names*. Special Publication 440. Washington, DC: National Bureau of Standards, December 1976.

Lanzi, Elisa. *Introduction to Vocabularies: Enhancing Access to Cultural Heritage Information*. Los Angeles: Getty Information Institute, 1998. (Designed to provide a basic understanding of the benefits of using controlled vocabularies in cultural heritage information contexts.)

Levenstein, Mary K., and Cordelia F. Biddle. *Caring for Your Cherished Possessions*. New York: Crown Trade Paperbacks, 1989.

Linker, Mike. *Managing Pests*. North Carolina Cooperative Extension Service, 2000.

Mailand, Harold. *Considerations for the Care of Textiles and Costumes: A Handbook for the Non-Specialist*. Indianapolis: Indianapolis Museum of Art, 1980.

Nicolson, Adam. *The Fire at Uppark*. London: The National Trust, Toucan Books Limited, 1990.

Ordoñez, Margaret T. *Your Vintage Keepsake: A CSA Guide to Costume Storage and Display*. Lubbock, TX: Costume Society of America/Texas Tech University Press, 2001.

Phipps, Elena. *Looking at Textiles: A Guide to Technical Terms*. Los Angeles: J. Paul Getty Museum, 2001.

Pinninger, D. *Pest Management in Museums, Archives, and Historic Houses*. London: Archetype Publications, 2001.

Robinson, Jane, and Pardoe Tuula. *An Illustrated Guide to the Care of Costume and Textile Collections*. London: Museums & Galleries Commission, 2000.

Standards in the Museum Care of Costume and Textile Collections. London: Museums and Galleries Commission, 1998.

Story, Keith O. *Approaches to Pest Management in Museums*. Washington, DC: Smithsonian Institute, Conservation Analytical Laboratory, 1985.

Thornes, Robin, with Peter Dorrell and Henry Lie. *Introduction to Object ID: Guidelines for Making Records That Describe Art, Antiques, and Antiquities*. Los Angeles: Getty Information Institute, 1999. (Excellent section on how to photograph objects. Originally came about as a way to systematically document objects so that, if stolen, the object can be easily returned to its rightful owner and a systematic description can be rapidly distributed around the world.)

Thurman, Christa C. Mayer. *The Department of Textiles at the Art Institute of Chicago*. 2nd rev. ed. Chicago: The Art Institute of Chicago, 1989.

Zorich, Diane M. *Introduction to Managing Digital Assets: Options for Cultural and Educational Organizations*. Los Angeles: Getty Information Institute, 1999. (Examines intellectual property rights and the desire of cultural heritage organizations to place their content on digital networks. Information in this report is based on a strategic analysis of US organizations. Museum Educational Site Licensing Project ended in 1997. Includes bibliography, glossary, and questionnaire for reviewing intellectual property management service providers.)

Index

Page numbers in *italic* indicate illustrations.